7 saving graces

Living Above the Deadly Sins

Steve DeNeff

wesleyan
publishing
house

Indianapolis, Indiana

Copyright © 2010 by Steve DeNeff
Published by Wesleyan Publishing House
Indianapolis, Indiana 46250
Printed in the United States of America
ISBN: 978-0-89827-420-2

Library of Congress Cataloging-in-Publication Data

DeNeff, Steve.
  7 saving graces : living above the deadly sins / Steve DeNeff.
     p. cm.
  Includes bibliographical references.
  ISBN 978-0-89827-420-2
  1. Christian life--Wesleyan authors. 2. Deadly sins. 3. Virtues. 4. Grace (Theology)
I. Title. II. Title: Seven saving graces.
  BV4626.D46 2010
  241'.04753--dc22
                                            2009053171

To my father.

Contents

Acknowledgements

The holiness preacher, Paul Rees, once said that he hated to write, but he loved to have written. Me too. Like him, I am a preacher first and a writer second. Many things I have written—this book being one of them—or would like to write, would never happen unless I was surrounded by a company of good and gracious people more capable than me. This book is largely the work of them who, first dreamed of it, and then provided the time and space for writing it. Let's roll the credits . . .

For almost nine years, the people of College Wesleyan Church have been my mentor, my inspiration, my laboratory, my support, my friend, my body, and my home. Their knowledge and experience is rivaled only by their grace. They have plenty. They have endured my shortcomings as a pastor so that I can focus more on preaching and writing. This book is the result of a study break first proposed by two members

(Ross Hoffman and Jackie White) and granted by the elders and deacons because they believe God has called them to serve the greater Church. Toward that end, many members have offered me their knowledge, their support, their company, even their home for awhile—whether in Colorado or Florida—so that I could write the book!

My staff (Thad Spring, Emily Vermilya, Charlie Alcock, and Jil Mazellan) has faithfully run meetings, programs, visitation—even interference—while I was finishing this manuscript and working on another. My executive team, David Drury and Judy Huffman, have encouraged me, humored me, sometimes prodded me, and advised me on most of these chapters. More than that, they have helped to shoulder the weight of College Wesleyan Church during a time of unprecedented growth.

The good people at the Wesleyan Publishing House have decided to take yet another chance on a book of mine. Don Cady has continued to support the promotion of the holiness message across the Church. Former editorial director, Larry Wilson, and I conjured up the idea for this book over two years ago, but it took the careful and gracious eyes of two editors, Kevin Scott and Rachael Stevenson, to make it happen.

I am most indebted to my family ("Uh oh, dad's writing again!") who has often started supper or started the movie without me. They have lived quietly (well, mostly!) under the strain of someone who is still writing what he hopes, one day, to have written. Nicholas and Ashley have grown into young adults since I last wrote, but they have remained close to us and are the joy of our lives. My wife, Lori, has given me her love, her wisdom, and her faith. She has loaned me courage and hope. Indeed, she has shown me all seven virtues—and added patience besides! She has heard every argument in this book (twice!) and has threatened to write it herself if I did not finish soon. Honey, I'm done. I'm hitting "send" in a few moments, and this time for good. I'll be home by six. Well, make that seven. All right then, seven-thirty. See you at eight.

—Steve DeNeff, Christmas Eve, 2009

1

In Pursuit of the Dream

A Passion for Wellness

D o you want to get well?"

The Son of God asked over two hundred questions in his ministry, which is remarkable when we consider that he, being omniscient, already knew the answers. This question, first uttered to a man paralyzed for thirty-eight years, was like all of the other questions Jesus asked. It was asked not because Jesus needed to know the answer, but because the person he asked did.

When Jesus asks a question, it does not matter who or how confident you are. You are probably not ready for it. What are you seeking? Where is your faith? Do you know what I have done for you? Who do *you* say that I am? What will a man give in exchange for his soul?

When anyone else asks you a question like this, the conversation is just getting started. But when it comes from Jesus, you can be sure the conversation has already been had in his mind.

Isn't that unnerving?

The Man at the Magic Pool

The paralyzed man was one of hundreds who lay around the magic pool called Bethesda, waiting for their luck to change. Every now and then, they believed, an angel would stir the waters, and when he did, the first one in the pool would be the lucky one. That person would be cured, relieved of pain, and free to start a new life.

But this man was paralyzed, or more accurately, "shriveled and wasting away."[1] To be paralyzed in his culture meant you had done something wrong. You had offended the gods. You were being punished. Those who walked by pitied and avoided you, but mostly they wondered what you did to deserve this.

Like the others at the pool, this man was reduced to begging for his very existence. He was self-absorbed, desperate, defined by his disease, and angry at those with better luck. He lived on a shoestring and took advantage of everything he could get—whether from the government, the temple, the rich, or relatives who felt sorry for him. Maybe he sometimes bought a lottery ticket as a votive offering to the god of chance, or maybe he stole from the rich, thinking it was only fair. He was a type of modern man: He waited, tried, failed, quit, and then tried again.

The man didn't really believe he would ever make it into the pool, and yet he couldn't leave it. What if something were to happen? What if he got lucky? So he hung around—hoping, but growing more cynical all the time.

Then, one day, a man approached him and uttered a stupid and offensive question: "Do you want to get well?"

Ask a stranger who is blind if he wants to see. Ask someone with Muscular Dystrophy or rheumatoid arthritis if she wants to get over it. What would her response be? She would almost certainly consider your question intrusive and judgmental, as if you were implying she didn't want to get better. Besides, it's none of your business. Proper etiquette is to say nothing. It is better to just smile and nod as you walk by and feel sorry for them.

Yes, the question could be considered offensive, and even more so because the day on which Jesus asked it was both a Sabbath and a festival day. Sabbaths and festivals were days of celebration and rest. Both were long-standing traditions that went back a few thousand years. Both were celebrated as part of the Jewish identity. Both traditions looked back, and both looked forward.

Sabbaths looked back to the days of Moses when God delivered his people and gave them the Law. Festivals, like the Day of Atonement or the feasts of tabernacles or Purim, all looked back to historic events that shaped Israel and proved her distinctiveness to God. A modern equivalent might be Independence Day—a celebration that looks back to the day when the nation was freed, even as it celebrates the ideals and dreams of that culture.

Sabbaths and festivals also looked forward to a day when the peace of Israel would be restored. Old Testament scholar Walter Brueggemann says they helped people "to imagine the world through the lens of that particular identity."[2] Festivals provided opportunities for the people of God to imagine again how everything would be in the end. Sabbaths and festivals spoke of order and peace, of hope and thanksgiving, and of joy. They were times to push reset, to pause and reflect on God's providence. Sabbaths and festivals were spent with family and were built around the quaint ideals of hope, contentment, and gratitude for all that was right. They were an opportunity to say, "It is well with my soul."

So Jesus deliberately chose a day when all was supposed to be well and entered a place where nothing was well and asked the question: "Do you want to get well?"

Strangely enough, the man never answered the question. He only complained that the other people were beating him into the pool whenever the waters were stirred. "The problem," said the withered man "is not me, but them. They are always cutting in line. They get all the breaks. They're the lucky ones." So he sat and listened every few days to someone else's testimony and watched someone else get healed. He was waiting on a dream. But maybe he was beginning to give up. Maybe he was growing cynical about all of these testimonies. Maybe he even hoped they would get sick again.

Still the question hangs in the air: "Do you want to get well?"

Well, do you? The question implies that there is such a thing as being well and that it is a condition quite different from your present one.

Getting Better vs. Getting Well

Jesus used a word that was different from the common word for healing. He used a word that means "whole" or "complete." There are several words for healing in the gospels, and each writer has his favorite. The most common word for healing—*therapeuo*—means to make better, to improve, or to get over what ails you. Jesus deliberately chose a different word—*hygien*—to show that he had something more than "getting better" in mind. The word Jesus used means "sound" or "reliable." It means to be "of good understanding . . . of good judgment . . . to be healthy [and] of sound mind."[3] It means "a proper balance of the whole."[4] In fact, he had wellness in mind.[5] Jesus was not asking the man if he wanted to get better; he was asking him if he wanted to get well.

Physicians know just what he means. Years ago, while I was in the hospital with a virus, two doctors came to my room. After spending a few minutes with me, they left to discuss my case. They didn't know it, but right after they left my room, I got out of bed and followed them down the hall to hear what they were saying.

"Well, his condition has certainly improved," said the one.

Then the other said something quite curious I have never forgotten: "Yesterday, he was over the virus, but today he is ready to go home."

The doctor was not referring to my state of mind. He was referring to my state of wholeness. He was talking about that point in the recovery process where relapse is no longer likely, where one's energy and drive has been fully restored just like it was before. Everyone knows it—from doctors to patients to insurance companies—a person may get better long before they are well.

When we get better, we are over our symptoms. But when we are well, we get rid of the disease. When we get better, we quit fighting or quit saying mean things with our tongues. But when we get well, we reconcile. We restore the love and trust and loyalty that we had with one another before the fight. We use our mouths to build people up. We reach a peaceful resolution to the conflict or, when we cannot, we bear up under the injustice and continue to love and pray for those who persecute us.

So the question "Do you want to get well?" is not a stupid question at all. Indeed, there are many who are defined by their diseases. Recently I read of a woman who made headlines for refusing to treat her child's deafness. Born deaf, like her mother, the child suffered a disease that doctors were certain they could cure with a simple surgery. But the mother refused, saying that deafness was not a disease but an identity. She said it was better for her child to remain deaf than to be subject to a world of distractions. To her, deafness was a better way to live, so she wanted neither pity nor help. She wanted only to be left alone.

Some who are spiritually deaf also defend their condition. They decide that, rather than be fooled by all the loud and confusing voices, they prefer to believe in nothing. They simply want to be left alone. They do not want to get well.

But most people do.

Most people really want to change. They want to be different; they just don't know where to begin. Most people are not rebellious so much as they are stuck. Many Christians were under the impression that once they were saved, all things would be new. But behold, all things are not new. Every day they wake up "saved" but with the same old instincts and habits. They are in the same tired relationships. It is not that they are faking their religion or even that they don't know how to change. It is that their old patterns are still too easy for them. Their old friends are still too familiar, their past too influential, their impulses too powerful, or their resolve too weak. Like the paralyzed man, they don't believe they will ever be cured, and yet they can't leave the pool. They act as if sin is too clever and too deep a problem to solve in this life. Yet there is something still in them that wishes they could somehow make it into the pool. All their lives they have heard someone else's testimony and seen someone else's miracle. So they hang around and get cynical while trying to retain hope.

Our culture is sick; even the physicians (theologians) themselves seem not to believe in wholeness anymore. They confess to sinning as though it were a badge of their genuineness. It is as though sin was a chronic disease—something you learn to live with and you treat for symptoms—and the church a mere hospice for patients who are terminal. Confession and penance are like pills a patient takes to treat the symptoms, but they do nothing for the disease itself. Many pastors and physicians are like pathologists who explain in great detail how the disease is killing us but have nothing to prescribe that kills the disease or even to keep it from flaring up again. If you doubt this, drive to the church nearest you and ask the pastor bluntly, "Do you think I will ever conquer sin in this lifetime?" As a doctor, he hates the disease and looks forward to a day when it is cured, but the harsh reality is that he has been up against it for so long that he is no longer optimistic. He has seen people who claimed to be cured, but who discovered later that they were only in remission. The sin came back later with a vengeance. Sadly, our society is so soured by these things, that even though we are hooked on getting better, we have lost the idea of what it means to be well. We are at the same time sinner and saint—always repenting.

Then Jesus comes strolling into our fatalism with his preposterous question: "Do you want to get well?

In our frustration, we command him to stop. "Do you know anyone who has stopped their sinning?" we ask, as though that were the end of the matter. Suddenly, our experience is the most important criteria. It's a fair question, but it isn't the first one to ask. There are others.[6] Even if you doubt, as many do, that a cure for sin is possible in this life, there is something inside you that won't let you leave the pool. Even as you grow cynical, you still wonder: Does Jesus mean what he said? Even if you can't be whole, do you still wish that you could? Does your craving for wholeness imply that there is more out there for you? Is it really like God to offer you something you cannot have? Is Jesus capable of giving you what he offers? Even if you were the first one in the world to get it, could Jesus do it for you if he wanted? Does he want to?

I am writing in part to say, "Don't give up the dream!" Stay near the pool. Keep asking the question. Don't let someone else's testimony make you cynical. Don't be critical of someone else's miracle. However long it takes, however frustrated you get, keep seeking your miracle. You probably need one. Miracles do not come at the whim of those seeking them, and they do not always come in a day. Miracles happen when Jesus "sees us," and they happen to people who, like the paralyzed man, have stayed near the pool a long time. They happen to people who cooperate with whatever God is already doing in their lives, people who are willing to forego any pleasure, pay any price, or start any habit that they might be whole again.

Are the Holy among Us Still Sick?

This book is devoted to people who, like me, have been sick long enough and want to be well. Though I come from the holiness tradition and am sympathetic to its doctrine of sanctification, I am not interested in simply re-stating the party line. Though I have a bent toward a more theological approach to things and even claim to be sanctified myself, I do not want to write a new theology or convince you of a second work of grace. I am asking if you want to be well—and that is a different question. As for me, I want to live and die a Christian, and I want to take as many with me as I can. It is not the goal of this book to stake out theological positions or to debate the meaning of the "baptism in the Spirit." I desire to see the effect of these things.

Theologically, I am somewhere between those who say you can never be well (in this life) and those who say they are well already. That is, I am well enough to despise my sickness, yet sick enough to call it something else. I believe in holiness—I understand it and I teach it—but this is no guarantee that I am holy. Even though I claim to be, the evidence does not lie in my claim but in the witness of God's Spirit and in those places where I live out that witness in the fruit of His Spirit. So whatever your persuasion, if your heart and hunger are as mine, then—for the next two hundred pages—give me your hand.[7]

The book is designed to look more closely at a simple pattern for spiritual transformation which, as Robert Mulholland has put it, is "the process of being conformed to the image of Christ for the sake of others."[8] It takes time and sacrifice and discipline but, as my friend Mark Wheeter says, "Is there anything else in your life that you can get good at by doing nothing? Why do you expect that in your spiritual life?"[9] I believe we are transformed by cooperating with the Holy

Spirit to overcome evil with good in our lives. As God infuses us with grace, we have the power to say no to ungodliness in all its subtle forms and to live upright and godly lives in this age (Titus 2:12). God's divine power gives us everything we need for life and godliness so that through his promises we can actually participate in his divine nature (2 Pet. 1:3–4). We can share God's attribute of holiness with him (Heb. 12:10). We can live as Christ to the world (Gal. 2:20; Phil. 1:21). For God did not call us to be impure but to live a holy life (1 Thess. 4:7). So no lasting change can occur without a sustained discussion about sin and grace, vice and virtue.

We will begin by defining *vice* (Chapter 2) and *virtue* (Chapter 3) and then, in the heart of the book (Chapters 4–10), discover how each of the seven deadly sins—along with its opposite virtue or saving grace—competes for the same space in our lives. One premise of this book is that by God's grace, we can develop our virtue even though we are better at vice. Though we are sinful from birth, we have inklings, longings, and strange little habits reminiscent of grace. We have distant memories of a better day we never had, like phantom pain from a limb that never was. Thus, another premise is that our trouble with sin is not only what it does to our chances of heaven but what it does to our potential on earth. In sin we have grown old and no longer know how to have fun. A third premise is that sin is a very old and clever adversary and it pursues sinner and saint alike. It is no respecter of persons but is always crouching at the door, masquerading as something else, even something virtuous. But a fourth premise is that sin can be mastered in all of its forms. It can be gotten over, cured once and for all by a grace growing opposite it. As each grace grows, it displaces the contrary sin. However, the opposite is also true. As sin grows, it pollutes the soil once fertile for grace.

As one who is holy yet still getting over his sickness, think of me not as a physician but as a fellow patient in the same hospital who, having been here awhile, has noticed some of the tendencies of our sickness and some of the patterns that lead to the cure. Along the way, I will share whatever I know of each and try to give general counsel that encourages and points toward wellness and life.

The feast of the Jews, the magic of the Greeks, the hope of all who lie helpless at the pool waiting for their luck to change is not found in religion at all. It turns out it is found in the one who is standing before you, perhaps even now, asking, "Do you want to be well?"

End of Innocence
The Persistence of Vice

The king cobra is among the most feared serpents in the world. Make him mad and he can uncoil his long body to stand one-third of it straight in the air to look you, fang-to-face right in the eye. Even if you like snakes, believe me, you want no part of this. One bite from him can deliver enough neurotoxin to kill you twenty times over, and within minutes. It can kill a full-grown elephant in just three hours. In fact, every year, in spite of our best antivenins, hundreds still die from his bite, quick as lightning and deadly. But the cobra is not the only snake whose bite is worse than its terror.

The black mamba is one of Africa's finest killers. It has the same amount of venom as the cobra with this distinction: It is the fastest of all serpents, moving twelve miles per hour at full throttle, and it is the most aggressive, at times even stalking its prey. It strikes without warning, and its bite is nearly always fatal. Without prompt medical attention, your chances of surviving a bite from the black mamba are nil. Unlike the cobra, it never bothers to look you in the eye. If you happen to wander by, it just nails you. Recently, one young Brit was nipped in the heel by an adolescent mamba and by the time he complained of the symptoms, it was too late. He died en route to the hospital. Another young man crawled into his sleeping bag without knowing a mamba had lodged itself at the foot. By the time his friends could pull him out, he was bitten thirteen times and lived less than thirty minutes.

The venom works on the victim's nervous system, affecting his vision and making him dizzy and numb. Then, when the toxins have taken hold, the victim is paralyzed and unable to defend himself. Soon after, he goes into convulsions. After about thirty minutes, he is comatose or dead.

Two Kinds of Sin

Sin is a snake bite. There is the part you notice (the bite), the part that keeps coming back (the snake), and the part that stays with you (the venom). You can shake off the bite and even kill the serpent, but it is not the serpent or the bite that gets you. It's what the serpent leaves behind. Sin is like that. It comes not only as a bite or a serpent, but as the lasting effect of both.

Augustine divided sin into two categories—actual sin and original sin. One is the bite and the other the serpent.

Actual sin is the sinning itself. It's what we do or fail to do. Like a bite, it's the part that hurts, the part you can see, the part that gets all the attention. The Bible has several lists of these sins, from the "six things the LORD hates" (see Prov. 6:16–17), to Jesus' list of things that "make a man 'unclean'" (see Mark 7:20–23), to Paul's three lists of sins whose doers "will not inherit the kingdom of God" (see 1 Cor. 6:9–10; Gal. 5:19–21; Col. 3:5–9). Actual sin is an addictive behavior— a short temper, a half-truth, a malicious word, a lustful thought, a sacrilegious joke. Actual sin is the "it" in "I did it again." It's the sin you hate to love—the habit, the weakness, the trap, the excess, the mistake you keep making, the hole you put yourself in. We all know the bite of lying, lusting, fighting, hoarding, or of simply doing nothing when more is required. We have all been bitten again and again.

But these days, we are far less familiar with the serpent. Original sin is what Augustine called the sin behind the sin. By that, he meant the part that keeps coming back, the evil that sees you before you see it, and that stalks you and nips at your heel. This is your bent for sinning, for continually committing the same sin. It is your tendency to put yourself in the center of your world and to pull all others to yourself. It is the desires and the evil thoughts that are in your heart long before you act on them. While there are many bites, there is only one serpent, and the more we are bitten, the more paralyzed and defenseless we become.

Traditionally, this is where schools of theology have parted ways. Some, like those in the holiness tradition, believe we can be free of both serpent and bite in this lifetime, while others, like those in the Reformed tradition, insist we can never be free from the serpent but only protect ourselves from the bite. To these good people, every new bite (or sin) only reinforces their suspicion that the serpent is still alive and well. Every failure only reminds them how futile their attempts at living a holy life are. One such reader of the magazine *Christianity Today* recently expressed his hopelessness like this: "I have been working and struggling against my personal sins for 46 years; so I conclude that the doctrine of entire sanctification is a sham, as phony as a $3 bill."[1] Apparently, someone told him entire sanctification would kill the serpent and there would be no more bites.

Maybe he consecrated his life and even professed to be sanctified. Maybe he even believed it for awhile, but now he is not so sure. He has been bitten again and again and has concluded the serpent (or sin) is alive and there is no hope of avoiding it. To be sure, there are many who claim to have killed the serpent (that is, who claim to be sanctified) yet continue to do what the serpent would do. How can they be sanctified when they still have so many problems? How can holy people do ungodly things?

Why Do Holy People Do Ungodly Things?

Perhaps there is yet another kind of sin called residual sin. Residual sin is like the venom the serpent leaves behind after the bite. It is the long-term effect of sin in our lives even after those sins have been confessed and cleansed. Like venom, residual sin affects our habits, personalities, behavioral patterns, mental processes, and worldview and distorts them—much the way snake venom distorts the neurological impulses of the body. In this sense, residual sin is still sin—in the proper sense—because it does everything sin does. It distorts our vision of God, it fetters our potential, it interferes with our relationships, it suppresses our impulse to worship, it blinds us to our own shortcomings, and that's just for starters. It is less visible than an act, yet more specific than a nature. It is an impulse or an intuitive response. It is a learned behavior.

Even after we have killed the serpent (or have been cleansed of our sinful nature) and shaken off the bite (or gotten over the sin), there are things like low self-esteem, laziness, stubbornness, foolishness, flippancy, and a restless or busy spirit that can damage us for the rest of our lives. These "toxins" are active and progressive. They intrude into our lives and debilitate us.

Like other sins, these toxins must be overcome. They will not necessarily send us to hell, but they might send a little hell into us. They will deprive us of the glory we had in the garden. They can tarnish the image of God. Through the serpent and the bite, all have sinned, and through the blood of Christ, all may be cured—but there is still the hard work of overcoming the venom the serpent left behind.

No single act by God or by man will get rid of this. It will take the two of us working together. Not even a sanctifying moment can cure us from the effects of the venom. We will not suddenly believe in things unseen or value others as much as we ought or become meek and merciful overnight. We do not suddenly like to be last instead of first or to give our hard-earned money to the poor. It is not our nature to trust instead of worry, to turn the other cheek, to rejoice while we are suffering, to give a soft reply to anger, or to value Scripture as much as we value gold. And yet, dare we say, we will never learn these things in this life? Must we wait for heaven to become what Jesus was on earth?

Why do holy people do ungodly things? Perhaps they suffer the residual, long-term effects of sin even after the sin has been taken away.

I have an acquaintance who says he is sanctified, yet he talks about himself all the time and always in the most boastful manner. He turns every conversation into an exhibition of some event in his life. Whatever has happened to you has happened to him first, only his version is more interesting (to him) than yours. He doesn't see it, but everyone else does. So guess what? They talk about him too, only they talk about his narcissism and not his sanctification. Now one Christian tradition says he is not really sanctified, even though he thinks he is. And another tradition says he is, even though he acts like he isn't. Who's right?

Perhaps there is another explanation that makes him more than forgiven, yet less than perfect. Perhaps there are triggers in this young man's life that leave him vulnerable to the annoying habit of talking about himself. One such trigger might be his personality or temperament. If he is strong-willed, he might have a tendency to be short with people or to ignore them. The same is true with all of us. If you are a passive person, you might hate confrontation. You might internalize your frustrations more easily than you talk about them, and this can make you vulnerable to bitterness. If you are a contemplative person, you might be a perfectionist. You might not affirm others as much as you ought, or you might be critical of them. There is nothing sinful about our personalities, at least not as God created them, but our personalities will certainly leave us vulnerable to sins that don't seem to tempt others.

Sometimes our history or personal experiences create learned behaviors that are negative, anti-social, or even sinful. Take my friend who always talks about himself. If he has a history of being ignored or overlooked as a child, it would not be uncommon for him to compensate for this deficiency by stumping himself. To be sure, Jesus was not boastful like this man, and so he is not like Jesus. But then, Jesus had a very different father, and sanctification itself cannot give this man a father or a past as good as Jesus'. He will have to learn it some other way.

Even more, sometimes our physical condition or limitations can become carriers of a sin that is not in us. For instance, when your serotonin level is low, you are likely to be depressed and, while neither low serotonin nor depression is sinful, either might make us vulnerable to despair or to worry or to fear. Personally, I have had diabetes for thirty-one years, and while it is under control, every now and then when my blood sugar is low, I will lose control of my emotions. I can become careless and obnoxious, or grumpy and critical, or sad and disoriented. While I may not choose to have these emotions—and they are not part of my normal state of mind—I have them nonetheless, and they can become quite bothersome to people who have to live with me. In this sense, they are not innocent and neither am I. But to say this can be cured with sanctification is simplistic and wrong-headed. Rather than consecrate them, I have learned to handle them by using a variety a measures to keep myself from hurting others.

We may be forgiven of our sins or even sanctified—as holiness people like to say—and never be rid of these proclivities because they are not the same as sin nor do we sin by having them. Indeed, not even sanctification can take them away. To be rid of them would not make us more human, but less, and yet they make certain sins more likely, even among the holy. Even when we are free from the power of sin, we will never be free from the temptation to sin, because sin can attach itself to one of these triggers and slip unnoticed into our lives.

The point is this: Rather than deny our sins, we need to develop a new sensitivity to sin in all of its forms. We need to remain humble, aware that Satan may at any moment use our vulnerabilities against us and sift us as wheat unless Jesus prays. We must learn to confess our sins and to set up virtues in the opposite direction.

But to do this, we would need a list of sins to confess. Fortunately, there is such a list and there has been for almost two thousand years.

The Story of the Seven Deadly Sins

The process of being converted—of getting rid of the venom of sin and restoring our health—has been called the "way of holiness" or the "way of perfection." In the early church, this way was divided into two parts: (1) the renunciation of sin and (2) the practice of virtue. Regarding sin, we were told to confess it and then to abandon it. Regarding virtue, we were told to produce it (see Matt. 3:8) and to "overcome evil with good" (Rom. 12:21). That was simple enough. But what "sins" should we confess? And how would we know they were sins? How could we abandon them when they seemed so natural?

As far back as the third century, a group of contemplative, devout hermits known as the Desert Fathers holed themselves up in the caves of Egypt to study the cure of souls. While few of these men were formally educated, they compiled their teachings into sayings or proverbs that were memorized and widely known as a rule or guide for living the holy life. To aid in the renunciation of sin, in the first part of the "way of holiness," they listed a catalogue of things one could do to get himself into trouble and for which he should repent. As you can imagine, there were lots of them. Years later, a couple of their monks classified these things into eight categories.

Evagrius Ponticus (A.D. 345–399), an educated and contemplative monk who lived with the Desert Fathers, created a list of "Eight Impure Thoughts" to aid his brothers in the arduous process of self-examination. Though he periodically edited the list, swapping one impurity for another, his list has remained pretty consistent to this day. It includes: gluttony, lust, greed, sadness, anger, sloth, vainglory, and pride. It is significant that, to Evagrius, these temptations were always thoughts and not demons or even deeds. The evil which the monk should resist did not come from outside or from the world but from within and dwelled primarily in the mind.[2] That we know of, Ponticus did not perceive of any particular order or precedence to the sins, but he did divide them into classes—those affecting the desire (gluttony, lust, and greed), those affecting the mood (sadness, anger, and sloth) and those affecting the intellect (vainglory and pride).

A few years later, one of Evagrius' disciples, John Cassian (370–435), had a series of private conversations with an abbot named Serapion about the subject of a devout life. Cassian wanted to further the ideals and methods of piety he had learned in Egyptian monasteries and make them available to more people. From these conversations, Cassian formed his own list of eight vices, which were very similar to Evagrius', only he called them "Principle Faults." To Cassian, the difference between vices and thoughts was a pretty big deal, for it moved Evagrius' list out of the mind and targeted certain behaviors. Sins were visible and tangible actions that could be seen. They were habits to be broken, not just urges to be controlled, and Cassian classified these habits into two categories: those that come from within (that is, they arise from purely natural desires, such as gluttony arising from natural hunger and lust arising from natural affection) and those that come from without (that is, they are foreign to our natural desires, such as covetousness or sloth). There were sins that required the body to commit them (such as gluttony and fornication) and sins that could be hidden in the mind (such as greed, anger, sadness, sloth, and pride). But behind the list was always the idea of helping Christians to recognize their sins so they could renounce them. Remember, this was the first half of their spiritual formation.[3]

A little more than a hundred years later, the church was in a moral crisis. During the time of Pope Gregory the Great (540–604), the sacrament of baptism was believed to be the line between sin and salvation. In addition to bringing people into the church, baptism served as evidence that their past sins were forgiven and their natures were changed. From that time on, they were expected to live different lives, even down to changing their occupations if necessary. At the very least, new converts were expected to abstain from sexual impurity, to denounce the excesses of wealth and to keep from swindling widows and orphans. Some professing Christians did these things while trying to maintain their relationship with the church. This was a serious problem for Gregory. How could believers continue to sin even after they were forgiven (or baptized)? What was the point of baptism if it did not lessen the impulse to sin? Of what value was the Christian community if its members behaved like the rest of the world? What should be done about the individual who persists in his sin? Gregory concluded there must be three essential elements in the sinner's repentance: confession (the acknowledgment of sin), contrition (godly sorrow over sin), and penance (good works done in love).[4]

But what should the sinner confess? For what should he do penance? To answer these questions, Gregory recovered the lists of Evagrius and Cassian and weaved them into his sermons on the *Morals of Job* which he intended as a guide to the church. Since he was no ordinary priest, but a pope, Gregory's teachings became standards for the whole church. Like Cassian, Gregory argued that there was a definite order to the sins, that one begat another, and that all began with pride, since it determined a person's relationship to grace, the greatest of all gifts. He added envy and eliminated sloth, combining it with "sadness" from the earlier lists. Finally, Gregory changed the name of these from "faults" to "sins." To Gregory, these were not flaws or infirmities, and they were not for monks alone. They were serious and they belonged to every member in the church. It was Gregory who first coined the phrase "Seven *Deadly* Sins." Next to the previous two lists, Gregory's looked like this:

Evagrius Ponticus	John Cassian	Pope Gregory
Gluttony	Gluttony	Lust
Lust	Lust	Gluttony
Greed	Greed	Sadness
Sadness	Anger	Greed
Anger	Sadness	Anger
Sloth	Sloth	Envy
Vainglory	Vainglory	Pride
Pride	Pride	

After Gregory, the list of deadly sins resurfaced in the writings of various spiritual advisors.

But in the middle ages, Thomas Aquinas (1225–1274) made spiritual formation a virtual science. He painstakingly distinguished between various types of sin and, like his predecessors, concentrated much of his energy on seven in particular, borrowing his list from Gregory. Aquinas put each in its appropriate category (whether mortal or venial) and provided his readers with remedies against them. Aquinas' work, included in his "Sum of Theology" (*Summa Theologia*), became the template for both church doctrine and pastoral counsel.[5]

Following Aquinas, the tortured poet Dante took Aquinas' version of the big seven and created a separate punishment in hell for each of them. In hell, Dante said, the proud would be broken on a wheel, the envious would have their eyes sewn shut, and the lustful would be smothered in fire, while the angry would be dismembered alive. Those who were gluttonous would be made to eat rats and those who were greedy would be boiled alive in oil. Some believe that due to his exile and rejection by many in the church, Dante assigned one of his enemy's faces to each of the deadly sins and thus began his vengeance in what is now known as *The Divine Comedy*.[6]

After the middle ages, a group of mystics resumed interest in the list of deadly sins, turning them into contemplative reflections—a means of assessing the amount of sin still hiding in our lives. One such writer, St. John of the Cross (1542–1591), wrote contemplations on each of the sins in his best known work, *Dark Night of the Soul*, which has become for many, including myself, a template for self-examination. Dividing our spiritual progress into three stages—beginner, progressive, and perfect—John of the Cross believed the capital sins (as he called them) were obstacles that prevented the beginner from developing in the virtues. Under the influence of the mystics, the deadly sins were more than a list of forbidden acts. They were living things. They moved, they evolved, and they stalked their prey. They were as wise as the serpent himself. The categories were made broader and more abstract. Pride was not just self-importance, as Evagrius taught, but the criticism of others who were slow in their devotion or becoming too angry and impatient with their own progress. Greed was as subtle as preferring cleverness over simplicity, and gluttony was being too chatty in confession.[7] By internalizing each of the deadly sins, the mystics merged the earlier concepts of "thoughts" and "faults" to make broad categories so that any devout Christian, if he was serious, could find one of them to confess.

Today the Catholic Church, which brought us the original list, has recently updated it in a much needed effort to revive our culture's sensitivity to sin and to encourage more of the faithful to attend confession. The New Seven Deadly Sins, as the pope has called them, include (1) bioethical violations such as abortion or birth control; (2) morally dubious experiments, such as stem cell research; (3) drug abuse; (4) polluting the environment; (5) contributing to the widening division between the rich and poor; (6) excessive wealth; and (7) creating poverty. These sins "have appeared on the horizon of humanity," said Pope Benedict, "as a corollary of the unstoppable process of globalization."[8]

Why the Seven Deadly Sins?

Nearly everyone has heard of the seven deadly sins, but most cannot name more than three (usually lust, anger, and pride), and the idea of avoiding them seems quaint, even silly. I mean who worries about sloth anymore? Greed actually motivates us and keeps the economy going. Our houses have gotten larger (30 percent), yet our families have gotten smaller.[9] We are saving less and gambling more. Forty-eight of the United States have some form of legalized betting.[10] Only thirty years ago, 15 percent of us were obese, but now a third of us are.[11] Almost half of the top selling CDs today include sexual content that is either "pretty explicit" or "very explicit."[12] Almost three-fourths (72 percent) of us have agreed with the statement, "I'm mad as hell and I'm not going to take it anymore."[13] Two-thirds of our television shows include violence, and children's programming is the most violent of all. Television exposes our children to over ten thousand acts of violence each year. By the time they are twelve, they will have witnessed twenty thousand murders and eighty thousand injurious assaults, and that does not include the violence they have seen, indeed helped to create, in video games.[14] Even religion has incorporated some of the deadly sins into a twisted gospel devoid of God's power. There is the gospel of self-esteem (pride), the gospel of prosperity (greed), the gospel of the conservative right (anger), and even the gospel of fitness and dieting (inverted gluttony).

David Kinnaman has noticed how these new morals have slipped into the lifestyles of many born-again Christians. Kinnaman compares the lifestyles of those aged twenty-five and under (called "Mosaics") with those in their thirties and forties (called "Busters") and observed:

> Born-again Christian young people are three times more likely to have had sex outside of marriage in the last month (*lust*) . . . five times more likely to have gotten drunk (*gluttony*) . . . and five times more likely to have purchased a lottery ticket (*greed*) . . . they use profanity in public (*anger*), view explicit sexual content in a magazine or a movie (*lust*), or say mean things about others (*pride*).[15]

I count five of the seven deadly sins in Kinnaman's short assessment. He writes, "Younger born-again Christians need to take an honest assessment of their lives and realize that they are increasingly poor witnesses of a life and mind transformed by their faith."[16] And this is exactly the point. The seven deadly sins, together with their corresponding virtues, provide a much-needed correction to the shallowness of modern spirituality. They offer a template for self-examination. They remind us of the reality of sin, of the ways in which we are not like Christ. They point to deep and hidden flaws we have long ago stopped looking for because we are either too tired or are defining deviancy down. The deadly sins remind us of everything Jesus was not, even though in his humanity, Jesus was everything we are.

Even more, the deadly sins are blunt reminders of how bad we are. So when I examine myself for a critical spirit or an ungrateful heart, the seven deadly sins stand there, arms folded, and wait for me to finish with my excuses, then remind me that my real problem is pride and that I have it in spades and that a spade is, after all, a bloody shovel. It is one thing to say that I do not compliment others enough, that I am too easily lost in my own things, that I have a discerning eye and high standards. But it is quite another to say that I am too proud. Without the reminder that these things are really sins, I would gladly confess my faults, because these days confession is thought to be as noble as virtue itself.

Finally, the seven deadly sins offer an outcome-based plan for spiritual formation. Too often, we judge our progress in holiness based on a series of inputs—a crisis of faith, a spiritual discipline, a class on discipleship, a catechism, or a spiritual director. We presume that because one has accomplished the input, the outcome has also occurred. To be sure, all of these inputs are very helpful in forming us into the image of Christ, but they are not the image itself. They are only a means to an end. We may never reach the end without them, but we may use them without reaching the end. Indeed, many have.

But the end of our faith, the salvation of our souls, is the actual conversion of our whole nature into the image of Christ. The end is a person that esteems others as more important than self. It is a content and generous heart. It is a soul that has taken ownership of the spiritual climate in his or her church; that has learned to wait on God; to see with faith, to rejoice in suffering, and to suffer with the world. Sometimes inputs create this kind of person and sometimes they don't. They are prompters or triggers; rituals that initiate a change and speak of something greater still to come. But they are not magic. Once we have consecrated our lives to God and availed ourselves of the means of his grace, we have still to do the hard work of helping God with the outcomes. God has called us to be holy, and holiness is an outcome. The seven deadly sins are simply one way of assessing our actual progress in it.

Still, holiness is more than the absence of sin. It is the presence of grace and virtue. It is putting on a new person created to be like God in righteousness. Yes, our study on the seven deadly sins is actually a study and pursuit of grace. Opposite of every vice, with which we are too familiar, is a magnificent grace for which we were made.

Flipping the Moon
The Power of Virtue

In the epic struggle between good and evil, it is striking how stubborn they are. Both of them, I mean.

"I did it again," says the man caught smoking marijuana in his garage. "I know better, but my life is so hectic, and I needed something to calm me down."

Another confesses his addiction to pornography. He is married and has not told his wife. "I love her," he says, "and I don't want to hurt her. Do you know what I mean?"

"Pray for me," says an athlete at a Christian university, "because I love God—I really do—but I also love women and I love to party. Do you know what I mean?"

Do you?

The Christian husband loses his temper and hits his wife, then tells her he loves her and won't do it again. Tomorrow he will buy her something nice as a form of penance.

The Christian mother screams at her children again, saying things that will mark them for life. But when she has calmed down, she takes them out for ice cream and buys them toys to make up for her failure.

The teenager who cuddles with his parents on the couch is capable, within the hour, of saying things about them the devil himself is too mannerly to say.

While most people notice the evil in what these people are doing, I am just as intrigued by their good.

"When I want to do good," said Paul, "evil is right there with me" (Rom. 7:21). Yet the opposite is also true: When we want to do evil, good will not leave us alone. We are just as inclined to confess our sins as we are to commit them. We speak of the problem of evil, but it is only because we are drawn to the power of good. Were we ever to give ourselves completely to evil, we would then speak of the problem of good.

This is an old problem. As far back as Aristotle, teachers warned our natural desires were mostly up to no good. The only way to overcome them, to become what Aristotle called the great-souled or high-minded person, was to pursue the virtues. Sigmund Freud's id and ego addressed the same idea. Robert Louis Stevenson called it *The Strange Case of Dr. Jekyll and Mr. Hyde*. J.R.R. Tolkien called it "Gollum." But to Paul, it was the good I want to do, but cannot.

We are caught between the powers of good and evil. Both of them are subtle, active, and persuasive powers that overpower us before we can resist. The husband who loses his temper, the woman who screams at her children, the teenager who smears his parents are all possessed by both evil and good.

Think of the man caught smoking marijuana. If he is good, then why is he addicted to pot? But if he is evil, then why does he "know better"? Why does he hide it or excuse it? If the young married man is good then why does he struggle with lust? But if he is evil, then why does he still love his wife? I believe the college student when he says he loves God as much as he loves to party. He is not lying; he is confused. None of these people have a reason to seek help, except for their instinctive desire to be free from their sins. They do not come to have their sins absolved. They are coming to be rid of them. That they keep sinning is evidence they are not so good. But that they keep coming is evidence they are not all bad. By the active grace of God, there is still some good in them.

Just this morning I received an e-mail from a man who is so ashamed of things he has done that he says he cannot confess them because people would kill him if they knew. Yet in spite of his apparent evil, he is still ashamed, and he has already begun his confession just by writing. The evil in him betrays the good, and yet the good in him is sorry about it. Last month I talked with a young lady who is in the middle of an affair. She is actively pursuing a married man and per-suading him to leave his wife and children and to marry her. Yet she tells me she really loves God, she wants to do what is right, and she is growing closer to God every day. She says she and the husband she has stolen "bring out the best in each other." She is good enough to seek the Lord, yet bad enough to terrorize a marriage.

In the past thirty years of pastoral ministry, I have become con-vinced of two things. The first is that most people really do want to be good. And the second is that they fail nonetheless. Think of New Year's resolutions. Every year, millions of us make them and yet, within a few weeks, we fail to keep them. Every time we want to do good, evil is right there with us. But alongside that evil runs a stream of God's renewing grace. Were it not for that grace, we could not love beauty or feel pleasure—or even the twinge of guilt. We could not feel the impulse for compassion, nor feel obliged to hide our dirty deeds. Simply put, even though we are better at being bad, we can usually see the good enough to crave it.

Now if this is our problem, then the way to begin our spiritual journey is by listing some of the God-given virtues that lie dormant in us.

What Is Virtue?

By virtue, I mean the God-given, grace-imparted capacity for goodness; the original condition in which we were made. Virtue is the specific way in which we bear the image of God. It is the scent of a flower called righteousness; the DNA of God's divine nature. "Virtue," said the German theologian Josef Pieper, "is not tame respectability and uprightness . . . but the enhancement of the human person in a way befitting of his nature; [it is] the most a man can be. It is the realization of man's potentiality for being."[1]

The word itself, *vir* or *virtus*, was used by the ancients to denote the sum of excellent qualities possessed by a man, including physical strength, nobility of character, soundness of mind, and integrity of conduct. The word *virtu* was borrowed by the French in the tenth century, and again by the English in the thirteenth century to denote the ways in which a man presented himself, or reproduced himself, in people around him or in his offspring.[2]

Aristotle was the first to comprise a list of virtues depicting the "great-souled" or "high-minded" man. Among these were four in particular that acted as a hinge (or *cardos*) for all the others. These became the four cardinal virtues: self-control, courage, justice, and wisdom.[3] To Aristotle, these were the steps toward happiness, toward a well-adjusted life. By practicing these virtues, along with the others he listed, Aristotle believed we could rein in our passions and gain mastery over the forces controlling us. By virtue, we learn to control our appetites and impulses. For fear, we learn courage; for greed, generosity; for self-indulgence, self-control; and so forth.

But later, when the Christians began to practice these virtues, they took on a different meaning. The early Christians believed the great philosophers (Aristotle, Plato, Cicero) were right about their use of virtues but wrong about their origin and nature. The Christian view of virtue is very different from the philosophers' in at least three ways.

First, virtues do not begin with man but with God. God is not the perfect version of whatever we consider a virtue to be—whether patience, kindness, generosity, or anything else—for we do not create God by throwing together a random list of virtues. Rather, each virtue is only a label for a small part of some quality that finds its perfection in God. We believe virtue has no meaning or place—indeed it cannot exist—apart from God. All virtue begins with, proceeds from, is perfected in, and leads back to God. Since this is true, we cannot decide on our own to practice virtue. We are capable of practicing only what God gives us through grace. God must capture our heart or all of our striving is in vain.

Second, virtue does not lead to salvation but flows out of it. To Aristotle, the way to be virtuous was to resist the extremes that were opposite the character we were trying to create.[4] In Christian thought, however, the practice of virtue does not lead to salvation. Why? Because underneath our virtue is still the matter of the heart. The heart wants what it wants. Once the heart sees what it wants, there is no talking it out. Even when we discipline ourselves, as many do, the heart still remembers, still imagines, still longs for and seeks that which we have forbidden ourselves to do. What is needed is a complete transformation, not only of our actions, but of our very desire. Only God can make the good life appealing to us. We may practice virtue, but it is all for naught until our souls are kissed by desire. Seek virtue, by all means, but seek it as an expression of a miracle named desire. First seek the miracle, then the virtue.

Third, virtue is more than morality; it is sanctification. If virtue is an expression of saving grace, then the practice of virtue in place of vice is the means by which we are sanctified. It is the quality that we are to possess "in increasing measure" (2 Pet. 1:8). It is the effect of holiness. It helps us define, in practical terms, how we participate in God's divine nature. To the ancients, virtues were steps on the road to happiness. But to the Christian, they are steps on the road to holiness. They are not the marks of a perfect man but the image of God reflected in imperfect men. The virtuous person always reminds you of God.

Sin: The Dark Side of the Moon

For a thousand years, the most common definition of sin has been "any want of conformity unto or transgression of the law of God."[5] This definition, made popular by the *Westminster Shorter Catechism*, is predicated upon a couple of things. First, it presumes the will of God, more than the nature of God, is the standard. Second, it presumes conformity is the goal. God is a king or a judge whose will is expressed in the Law. We are his subjects, created to do his will, and sin occurs when we fail to conform to this. Sin is disobedience. It is a transgression or a crime against his authority.

This view of sin grew out of an earlier emphasis upon pride as the chief of all sins and came to influence many of the most popular theologians throughout history. The Reformed theologian, John Calvin, wrote that in Adam we "*revolted* from God's authority, not only because we were *seized* by Satan's blandishments but also because, *contemptuous* of the truth, we *turned aside* to falsehood."[6] Even John Wesley, who disagreed with Calvin about many things, agreed that the essence of sin was pride that was expressed in our rebellion. Although he insisted that unbelief came first: "Unbelief begot pride: She (Eve) thought herself wiser than God . . . It begot self-will (She was determined to do her own will) . . . It begot foolish desires and completed (them) all by outward sin."[7] In his sermon on the "Fall of Man," Wesley said Adam "chose to do his own will rather than the will of his Creator; he was not deceived but knowingly and deliberately rebelled against his Father and his King."[8] To these men, sin was not an accident. It was not a flaw or an excess of our otherwise good character. It was pre-meditated. It was sin in the first degree, with intent to unseat the Sovereignty of God. Contemporary theologians call it cosmic treason or self-worship or a deliberate independence. Some have called it the wanting of one's own way.

While there is much good in this explanation for sin and salvation, and while millions have come to be saved while hearing it, it is not the whole story or the last word on sin. Like other doctrinal words, sin has many definitions but always the same effect: It separates us from God. For the remainder of this chapter, let's explore another definition of sin using a model and a couple of metaphors that helps to explain the forces of good and evil always at work in us: Why do we hate sin, and why can't we leave it alone?

Perhaps sin is the flipside of virtue. Perhaps our virtue is merely the reflection of some quality that already exists in God. As bearers of God's divine image, perhaps every good thing we admire and are striving to become begins with, proceeds from, and is perfected in God. As the moon merely reflects the sun but cannot create light on its own, perhaps all our virtue is merely a reflection of something that is true of God. Then, if our virtue is like the moon's reflection of the sun, perhaps our evil—or our sin—is the dark side of the moon. That is, with every virtue comes a corresponding sin or vice that mimics the virtue and turns it inward upon itself. To overcome the sin, we must isolate the virtue most opposite the sin—the one that the sin corrupted—and grow it. Then our vices will give way to virtue. Contrary to what ancient philosophers believed, virtue is more than just a way to conquer our vice. Perhaps virtue comes first. Maybe it is as old as the garden.

Why Does God Forbid Sin?

When you begin to think of vice and virtue in this way, you start forming new ideas about why God forbids sinning. It is not because he is opposed to our pleasure. It is not because the sin is in violation to his will; for the will of God, like the will of man, does not come out of thin air. It is based upon something deeper, like his nature. The mystery of the gospel, the profound truth that goes beyond forgiveness, is that God is trying to give his nature to us. That is the reason for the Law. Sin is forbidden because it is always inconsistent with these two things: his nature and our potential.

Inconsistent with God's Nature

It is inconsistent with his nature because it is not the way he is. God is good and true and beautiful, and the law is a photograph of this. Think of the Ten Commandments. By his nature, God keeps his vows, so we must not commit adultery. He gives life, so we must not kill. He provides, so we cannot steal. He is the truth, so we will not bear false witness. He satisfies, so we will not covet. Indeed, we must have no other gods before him because, in fact, there are no other gods before him. What he tells us to do comes easy for him because it flows out of his nature. The degree to which it comes hard for us is the degree to which we are not yet converted, whether we are Christians or not. God's desire is for his people, not only to keep his law, but to bear his image.

Inconsistent with Our Potential

Sin is also inconsistent with our potential. It is out of order with the way we were created. Originally, God made us innocent and free and unselfish. He created us to enjoy all that was good and beautiful. That image, however, was lost in the fall. But on the day we first repent,

God, who has never lost sight of our potential, begins the long and arduous process of converting us back to the image we had and lost in the garden. That we had it once and that we saw it again in the full humanity of Jesus is solid evidence that it is possible in this world, in spite of how cynical many have become. Our desire to be good and our talk of getting better (as opposed to getting worse) are evidence that, even though it is still ahead of us, this goodness, freedom, and innocence are there to be had, however long the process, however high the price. To quit on this vision, just because it is difficult, is quitting on the vision of what we had as much as it is quitting on the vision of what we can still become.

I have some friends who like to restore old cars. Most of them do so, not because they hate new cars, but because they are naturally drawn toward classics. When they begin the process, they go shopping for a clunker, and when they find the one they want, they will always drop more money on it than it is worth—at least in my opinion. But that is because they are buying its potential. Not long ago, Marvin invited me into his garage where he said he was hiding a gem. All the way from the house to the garage, he boasted about his 1964 Pontiac GTO. It was fire truck red, he said, and would go from zero to sixty in a few seconds. "Just wait until you see it." But when he opened the door, what I saw was something far different. There on the floor was his "red hot" GTO in a thousand pieces, each one carefully dissembled by him and set into groups, awaiting its day with Marv. On the wall was a photo of a 1964 Pontiac GTO, fire truck red, completely restored to its original condition.

"What do you think?" he said.

"Well, I'm speechless!" The look on my face gave me away. This was no classic. This was not even a car. It was a piece of junk—in fact, a million pieces of junk—and I didn't have the nerve to ask him what he paid for it.

But before I could find a diplomatic way to tell him, Marv moved from one section of junk to another, calling each piece by name and telling me how he was going to put them together to create—or actually to re-create—something I would recognize and admire in the end.

"How long have you been working on this?" I asked.

"A long time," he said, "but I'm in no hurry. I work on it a little here and there, whenever I have time. It's coming along."

Though I could not see why, Marv was immensely proud of his classic car, broken as it was to smithereens. Even though he was very aware of its current condition (and he certainly knew better than I did what was wrong with it), he had never forgotten its potential. On the day he bought it, he had a mental picture of what that clunker would look like, and that's why he paid more than it was worth. That's why he bragged about it all the way to the garage, speaking of its future as though it had already happened. That's why he was so hard on it every time he went to work. He would take the thing apart and notice every little flaw, then go after it with a vengeance—not because he was mad at the car for being broken, but because he loved the car and knew its true potential. Whenever he would rifle through magazines and pin pictures of a 1964 Pontiac GTO on the wall, he would remind himself of that car's future. But he would also be reminded of its past. For the future of any classic is only its past. In that sense, Marv was never creating something new, something previously unheard of; so much as he was restoring what was lost. When he is done, it will not be a freak. It will be an original; a classic. And there is not just one kind of classic, but many. To convert his 1964 Pontiac GTO into a 1967 Ford Mustang would be, not only impossible, but foolish.

Perhaps God posts a picture on his fridge of what you will look like once he has finished restoring you. For this reason, he paid more to get you than you were worth. For this reason, he brags about you to the angels: "Have you considered my servant? There is no one on earth like him" (Job 1:8). For this reason, he goes after your sin with a vengeance, not because he is mad at your sinning, but because your sinning is inconsistent with the picture he has of your past and your future. So Paul said we "press on to take hold of that for which Christ Jesus [has taken] hold of [us]" (Phil. 3:12).

Sin, like rust, only plays off of the very virtue it destroys. The virtue was given in the garden while we were good. Sin only offers a fast and easy way to become what God has already promised we shall be. This means we can start with our sins—each of them, all of them, or just the one we commit everyday—and if we look behind them, we will find the benefit we really desire. Most of the time, God has already granted it in some other way. In other words, we seldom sin for the sake of the sin. It is always for the benefit we think the sin will deliver. The great irony—the thing that makes everyone in heaven wonder and everyone in hell laugh—is that, in most cases God has already granted the very thing we are sinning to get. All of the people we know who have died, whether they are in heaven or in hell, already know this. For many in heaven, it was their greatest surprise, and for many in hell, their greatest regret.

The Displacement Theory

So long as we have a virtue, we will never be free from the danger of vice. But take heart, because they always travel in pairs—good and evil, virtue and vice. Wherever we find a vice, there is somewhere nearby a virtue. By God's grace, that is our hope! Just as a vice can destroy our virtue, our virtue can overcome our vice; for, as the ancients used to say, "Contraries are cured by their contraries." This is the displacement theory, and it has been a fresh wind across the barren lives of many who struggle with sin every day. We cannot just detach ourselves from our sins. With God's help, we must displace our sins with their corresponding virtues. If we do, the sin will dry up and go away and the beauty of the classic—always in God's mind and always in our future—will begin to glow again.

Now, enter our sins. For each of the seven deadly sins, the early Christians devised a contrary virtue. For pride, they sought humility; for greed, generosity; for lust, chastity; for anger, patience; for gluttony, abstinence; for envy, kindness; and for sloth, diligence. It was a plan for spiritual formation. With this grid, they would renounce sin and practice virtue. They knew what sin to confess and what virtue to put in its place. It was a brilliant idea.

The only trouble is that it didn't work. Legion is the stories of early saints who took vows of poverty but hid their gold in the fields outside the monastery. Others took vows of chastity yet sired several children with more than one woman. Some sought to gain mastery over one vice, like gluttony, and ended up stuck with another, like pride. There was no getting over it.

Even today some insist we will always struggle with sin and will lose much of the time. But perhaps the way to be free from sin is to practice a different set of virtues. If patience doesn't cure anger, nor chastity lust, nor generosity greed, this does not mean that anger, lust, and greed are beyond cure. It only means that patience, chastity, and generosity are not the way to do it. These virtues seem only to suppress the sin. Perhaps there are other virtues we may use.

Fortunately, the Church has a longstanding list of virtues that go back to the fourth century. This list was comprised by Ambrose, a bishop from Milan. Ambrose believed God imparts three cardinal virtues at the time of our conversion: faith, hope, and love. Then, borrowing from the work of other philosophers, he incorporated four other natural virtues—justice, wisdom, courage, and self-control—into his list and insisted God made each one possible.[9] This list of virtues appeared many times over the next sixteen hundred years in the writings of theologians and mystics and saints. Sometimes they were listed alongside certain sins, but nearly always they were offered as a means to strengthen the soul of a person so they were able to overcome sin.

Alongside our study in the seven deadly sins, I want to take up the study of these seven virtues, or "saving graces" as they are sometimes called. If sin is only the dark side of the moon—that is, the flipside of God's virtue reflected in us—then perhaps if we develop our virtue, we can deprive the sin of its appeal.

Pharmacologists tell us the cure for every disease is already somewhere in the world, even somewhere nearby. All that remains is to discover it, harvest it, distill it, and convert it into medicine so it can be used for the treatment of specific diseases. In other words, the same earth that comes with all of these diseases also provides us cures. The trick is in matching them, the disease with its cure. I wonder if our trouble with so many sins is that we have tried to resist them with treatments that are impotent to cure them. I wonder if the cure for the seven deadly sins is the seven saving graces. Even more, I wonder if there is a grace to counter every sin.

Deadly Sin	Traditional Virtue	Saving Grace
Pride	Humility	Wisdom
Greed	Generosity	Hope
Lust	Chastity	Love
Anger	Patience	Justice
Gluttony	Abstinence	Self-Control
Envy	Kindness	Faith
Sloth	Diligence	Courage

Just as disease and cure may grow in the same earth, perhaps vice and virtue grow in the same garden called Eden. Following the order provided by the Roman Catholic tradition, let's look at each of the seven deadly sins, together with the virtues they distort and the saving graces God provides to overcome them.

Let us begin with an unyielding pursuit of virtue. Let us take possession of our souls and, by God's grace, walk into the things God has intended from the garden of Eden to the present day. Only by grace will we grow in our virtue and discover, in the end, there is nothing left for vice.

First Class Way of Life

Wisdom in Place of *Pride*

When Diogenes the Cynic showed up one day at Plato's house, he was disgusted to find a new luxurious carpet on the floor. To show his contempt, he wiped his feet on Plato's new carpet saying, "Thus do I trample upon the pride of Plato."

"With even greater pride," said Plato under his breath.[1]

Of all the sins, pride alone has the dubious advantage of making everyone sick except the one who has it. How else could an evil that provides so little pleasure have lasted, indeed flourished, as long as pride? It is because the only one who can name it cannot even see it. To them, it is always something noble. Pride wears, as its self-defense, a shiny armor that not only makes the one inside too confident, but easily deflects any attempt to confront it. It is impervious to everything from the outside. You've noticed this. When you first see it in someone else, you dare not say anything. You cannot preach to it, pray with it, or even mention it at all. It just will not listen. Indeed, it cannot, for pride is deafness of the soul. So if you are proud, think of this as the perfect chapter . . . for someone else!

What Is Pride?

Winston Churchill, considered by some to be among the three most significant people of his generation, was apparently every bit the legend in his own mind. According to one biographer, following an argument with his personal attendant, Churchill barked, "You were very rude to me," and, forgetting his position for a moment, the attendant fired back, "Yes, but you were rude, too." Churchill paused, then said in a calm voice, "Yes, but I am a great man."[2]

Indeed, the place where pride is most rampant is not in hell, where people know their position, but in the halls of power, where they don't. Condemning the proud monk in his day, Evagrius wrote that pride "induces the soul to refuse to acknowledge that God is its helper and to think that it is, itself, the cause of its good actions."[3] Augustine said pride was turning away from God and toward ourselves. Pride, he said, is like fornication. In pride we seek a glory in relation to ourselves that can only come from our relation to God. "The soul is guilty of fornication when it turns away from Thee and seeks (Thee) apart from Thee, and seeks what it cannot find pure and untainted till it returns to Thee."[4] In seeking to become more, we are fooled into becoming less. Pride diminishes us by separating us from the One in whom we have our being and convinces us there is more glory to be had in comparing ourselves with others than in losing ourselves in him. For Pope Gregory, sin was a virtual family tree, each with its own branches, and pride was the stubborn root that nourished them all. From pride came the forbidden fruit of vainglory, and from vainglory these seven other branches grew: "disobedience, boasting, hypocrisy, contentions, obstinacies, discords and the presumption of novelties."[5] Do you recognize any of those?

Like all deadly sins, pride comes as a bite, a serpent, and venom. When we are bitten by pride, we drop names or boast or talk over people. We become obstinate or rude or critical of others. We say "I know, I know" to everything someone tells us, as if we have heard nothing for the first time, and what is more, we cannot be wrong. We cannot even be right graciously. We leave conversations—and replay mental videos—worrying about what we said, how we sounded, how we looked, and what others were thinking about us. We worry a lot about appearances. We get self-conscious. We think mostly about our own agenda, like the nervous father who waited in a room down the hall, pacing back and forth, while his wife suffered through labor to give birth to their first child. When the nurse appeared to announce, "It's a girl!" the young father exclaimed, "Thank God; she will never have to go through what I have gone through tonight!"

Like the Pharisees, proud people exaggerate or lie to promote their own agenda (Matt. 23:27–32). Like Saul, they hold onto their positions long after they can still do them, simply because those positions belong to them, or because they have earned them (1 Sam. 15:24–31). Like Uzziah, they blur the lines between the sacred and the mundane (2 Chron. 26:16–20). Like Hezekiah, they show off in public what God has given them in private (2 Kings 20:12–19; Isa. 39:1–7). Like Nebuchadnezzar, they relish their accomplishments too long, or take credit for what other people have done (Dan. 4:28–32).

As a serpent (or a nature), pride makes us think we are separate from others. It thrives on comparison and competition. We know we are good at something because we have noticed others are not as good. And this is fair enough. But the road from self-discovery to self-absorption is a gradual one, with potholes of conceit, each without a bottom. We start by wondering who we are, and then by wondering who others are, and before we know it, the game is on. We are a little brighter or maybe not as pretty. We are a little quicker on the draw or maybe not as deep. That person does it better than me, but this person is a little worse, thank God. Then, to make matters worse, the serpent will mask itself as pity or love. It will not mind if we help another person so long as we are always reaching down to do it. In this way, do the proud "help" one another at work or "support" one another on the team? In this way, do they give to the poor or take up the fight of a minority? In this way, do some "love" their spouses who are, God bless 'em, so far behind spiritually? In this way, do the old patronize the young—not as leaders who are equal to them and surely not as saviors who could actually right the organization, but as novices or interns who, bless their hearts, have a lot to learn? In this way, do the young humor the old, not as giants upon whose shoulders they hope to stand, but as predecessors to themselves, mere presages to their own highness? One valedictorian at an Ivy League school told his classmates all of history was leaning forward, looking into the present day, waiting for this class to arrive. He could have titled his speech, "The world's ten greatest men, and how I picked the other nine!" It is hard to imagine an ego so large and uninformed coming from, of all places, a university.

As venom, pride deadens the ache of our low self-esteem and makes us feel better about ourselves. It adapts to any personality and attaches itself to any virtue so that even the most pious person and the most selfless act are vulnerable. Proud people will often notice the humility in another person and try to imitate it themselves, because they imagine how others would hold them in high regard if they were humble. In this sense, pride actually encourages us to develop other virtues so long as people notice and so long as we enjoy those virtues for ourselves. We may speak with the tongues of men and of angels or give all our money to the poor. Pride does not care, so long as we are asking how it looked, how it made us seem to those we hope were watching. But the hallmark of pride as venom is this: It deadens us to our own flaws and makes us hyper-sensitive to the flaws of others. We "love humility and hate pride . . . only in other people," wrote William Law, "for we never once in our lives thought of any other pride than that which we have seen in other people."[6]

Ouch! And if that's not enough, read the rest:

> The fuller of pride anyone is himself, the more impatient he will be at the smallest instances of it in other people. Reckon your-selves humble only so far as you impose every instance of humility upon yourself and never call for it in other people.[7]

In fact, said C.S. Lewis, "if you want to find out how proud you are the easiest way is to ask yourself, 'How much do I dislike it when other people snub me, or refuse to take any notice of me?'"[8]

The French mystic Frances de Sales observed that lots of people will minimize their accomplishments until you agree with them:

> We often say that we are nothing, that we are misery itself and the refuse of the world but we would be very sorry if anyone took us at our word or told others that we are really such as we say. On the contrary we make a show of flying away and hiding ourselves so that people will run after us and seek us out.[9]

No wonder the ancient church called this *superbia*—an insatiable desire to look good, a propensity to sell ourselves, to promote our image, and to cast ourselves in the most positive light. A little of it is necessary for other things like dignity and ambition, but a little goes a long way, and most of us have more than we need.

Where Does Pride Come From?

Pride is not, as many imply, an act of sheer rebellion so much as it is the duping of a cavalier soul in pursuit of something good. Like all other sins, it feeds on virtue. For instance, our virtue is that we are made a little lower than the angels, and pride will distort this to mean we are a little higher than everything else. It will pervert our instinct for innocence into an ugly refusal to admit we are wrong. In our desire to improve lies the temptation to become more than we ought. We resist our limitations but not because we are rebels. More often it is because we are fools.

Let's go back to the garden of Eden, to the genesis of trouble, and put ourselves in the story. In the beginning, we were part of one another in intimate and covenantal ways that have long been lost. One of us (Eve) was made from another (Adam) and yet was separate from the other. It was as if the one was completed by the other just as the other was dependent upon the one. Neither was the product of the other, and yet neither was complete without the other. Each was him- or herself, and yet each was wrapped up inside the other, identified by the other and belonging to the other, and our identity was based not on our similarities but on our differences.

But in that moment, when we first desired more for ourselves than we were destined to be (remember, "You will be like God," Gen. 3:5), we distinguished ourselves and separated ourselves, then protected ourselves by seeking to preserve our own interests.[10] After this, we are no longer looking out for the other nor is the other looking out for us. Each of us is looking out for ourselves.

In pride, we have turned into ourselves and away from others. The one for whom it was not good to be alone, indeed who was made for others, was alone again. Even though we are surrounded by others, working with others, depending on others, or even married to another, we are our own person. We think of no one. We look out for no one.

We belong to no one quite like we belong to ourselves. We are alone because all others, whether our family or our priest, are there to serve one of our interests. This is the root of pride, and it has the power to distort every other virtue by turning them into something that reminds us of heaven, but comes straight from hell.

Saving Grace: Wisdom

Traditionally, we have thought of pride's opposite as humility, believing the more humble we are, the less proud we will be. But this does not always work, as many who have tried will tell you. It is like telling a deaf person to listen to you. To the degree he can hear you, he isn't deaf. To the degree he is deaf, he can't hear you, and so he won't listen. He needs to have a little of whatever you want him to have, or he will never have any. If we who are proud could be humble, even in the slightest degree, we would not be proud—not for long anyway—because we would find true humility more satisfying than our pride.

In the Bible, we learn what pride really is and how to overcome it. We are offered a glimpse at its underbelly and then told how to displace it with something even greater than humility. Throughout the book of Proverbs, we are introduced to two women and told to avoid one and to marry the other. The one is Folly, and the other is Wisdom. These two qualities are, for some reason, personified as women and contrasted throughout the book (for example, see Prov. 9:1–18).[11] The beauty of one (Folly) is her pleasure and her relentless appeal to our senses. See Folly for a good time. The beauty of the other (Wisdom) is her character and her good health over the long haul. See Wisdom for a good life. Most of us are torn between these two women—one that is bad for you but naturally appealing, and the other that is good for you but naturally less appealing . . . at least until you are cured.

From reading Proverbs with these two women, we discover a couple of things about conquering pride. One is that the root of pride is not overconfidence, but folly. No amount of confidence is too much so long as we can handle it. If we can't, then any is too much. The real cause of our pride is the failure to see ourselves as we really are.

I'm thinking of the man who pushed his way to the front of a long line at the Denver airport, insisting he be served first.

"I have to be on this flight," he said, "and it has to be first class."

"I'm sorry," said the woman at the counter, "but I have to serve these other passengers who were here first. I'll be with you in a moment."

The man became angry and refused to move. "Do you know who I am?" he bellowed, in a voice loud enough to be heard by everyone at the gate. But the woman was unimpressed. She calmly grabbed the public-address microphone and, in a voice that could be heard across the terminal she said, "May I have your attention please? We have a passenger here at the gate who does not know who he is. If anyone here can help him with his identity, please come to the gate at once." As the man retreated to his rightful place at the back of the line, the people in the terminal burst into applause.[12]

To know who we are—to have someone help us with our identity—this is the way to wisdom. Bernard of Clairvaux said it was to recognize our unworthiness because we know ourselves.[13] Folly, on the other hand, is the separation of our true selves from reality. It is to revolt against our boundaries—to refuse to get old, or to refuse to get sick, or to refuse to be wrong, or to not take our losses gracefully. Folly is the dissonance between the person we pretend to be and the one we have always been. The proud person is not one who thinks highly of himself, but one who thinks more highly of himself than he ought (see Rom. 12:3); who thinks his achievements are better than they are; who thinks his position is more important than it is; who thinks there are more people watching than are; who thinks his stories are better than yours and whose words are legendary in his own mind. He does not think this because he is proud. Rather, he is proud because he thinks this. His folly comes first. If he knew the truth, he would not be proud. His pride, then, is only the symptom of his madness. With folly, he refuses to accept his limitations. He won't play by the rules because he is somehow above them. He scorns tradition. He condescends on the elderly. He ignores the work others have done. According to Proverbs, we walk with folly when we think or act in a way that is inconsistent with what heaven already knows to be true.

Thus we do not conquer pride by trying to be humble. We conquer pride with wisdom. If pride comes from one woman (Folly), humility comes from the other (Wisdom). Humility is the palpable logic of people who are in their right mind. Thus, the belligerent man in the Denver airport does not need to be criticized or mocked to bring him down a peg or two. He needs only to be put in his proper place—to be told he is no more important than anyone else—and if he is humiliated by this, it is not because the woman made a spectacle of him on purpose. It is because he learned, in front of the very audience he was trying to impress, he was not as important as he thought.

When we are wildly successful, we do not temper our success with criticism or the caveat, "Don't get a big head!" This only deprives us of enjoying our accomplishments and makes us clamor for the attention we think we deserve. Instead, we need to acknowledge that others have contributed to our success and that we owe them. If we are placed into positions of power, we don't need to be insulted to stay humble. We need only remember that not everyone knows us, and even if they do, it won't be for long, for "as for man, his days are like grass, he flourishes like a flower of the field; the wind blows over it and it is gone and its place remembers it no more" (Ps. 103:15–16). We say this, not just to keep ourselves humble, but because it is really the truth. It is what heaven already knows. As the old saying goes, we would worry less about what other people think of us if we only knew how seldom they do. Just as folly acts against the things that are true, wisdom acts in accordance with them. It gives to things the importance they have in reality. As the sign on the door of a child's tree fort put it, "Nobody act big; nobody act small; everybody act medium." Wisdom acts medium because it knows we really are medium. That is how we were made.

The Bible detests pride but, in the end, does not call for us to merely act humble. It calls for us to seek wisdom. The more wisdom we practice, the less of pride we will see. But how do we bring wisdom back into our lives? By now, the answer must seem self-evident but let's summarize it in a few simple steps.

The Practice of Wisdom

If pride is the result of turning away from God and becoming less real, then wisdom begins by returning to God to find our true selves.

To return, we must learn what it means to fear God for "the fear of the LORD is the beginning of wisdom" (Ps. 111:10; Prov. 9:10; "knowledge," Prov. 1:7). Why? This idea, more than any other, keeps us in our place. Out of this simple truth—God is God and we are not— flows a steady stream of humility. Yet how often do we try to control what only God can control? How often do we judge what only God can judge? If we can bring ourselves to admit this, obvious as it is, perhaps we can admit other limitations as well.

There are several ways to learn new reverence for God, and each of them is an opportunity to see ourselves in the proper light. We may discover him in creation by walking through his theater, looking at the creation he has formed with his hands.

President Theodore Roosevelt had a routine habit, almost a ritual. Every now and then, along with the naturalist William Beebe, he would step outside at dark, look into the night sky, find the faint spot of light at the lower left-hand corner of Pegasus, and one of them would recite: "That is the Spiral Galaxy of Andromeda. It is as large as our Milky Way. It is one of a hundred million galaxies. It is seven hundred and fifty thousand light years away. It consists of one hundred billion suns, each larger than our own sun." There would be a pause and then Roosevelt would grin and say, "Now I think we feel small enough! Let's go to bed."[14]

Creation can do that. If you wrestle with pride, you do not need someone to tell you to be humble. You need only to stand next to a mighty waterfall and try to have a conversation, or to stand on the edge of a vast canyon and try to throw a stone across.

Historians tell us the Greeks hardly knew of humility. Perhaps they dared not give themselves a God who was greater than man because to do so would only make man as small as he really is. Their deities were only gods who acted like men. Why shouldn't their men be mortals who acted like God? But the simple reminder that God is in heaven and we are on earth will keep us in our place.

Second, to learn wisdom, we must turn toward others. It is a strange paradox. Those who worry the least about their self-worth have the most. In losing themselves, they have found themselves. In falling to the ground to die, they are yet alive in each of us—only, being dead, they cannot tell it.

If pride has come by shutting others out, it will leave as we invite them back in. But if we invite them in only to get them interested in us, we prove our problem is worse than we thought. No, we must get genuinely interested in them. We must actively listen to their stories and take up their trivia. Are they really that boring? Or are we really that proud? Stuck on our own agendas, as we have been for years, it is hard to know the difference. Right here it gets even harder. We must learn the habit of asking, "What is it like to be the other person?" and "What do I have, right now, that they need the most?" Then do it, or say it, or give it, or call for it—anything it takes. As a friend of mine once told me, "The two most important people in the world, at any moment, are God and the person in front of me right now. The question is never 'What would Jesus do?' but rather, 'What would *you* do if you knew the other person was Jesus?'" For all we know, it is!

The third discipline we must learn is to follow a leader. Proud people are still capable of learning, but they never tell that to their teachers. They have an annoying habit of saying or thinking "I know, I know" to everything you teach them. They lean on their own understanding. But wise people know they do not know; they will risk appearing a little ignorant now in order to be smarter later. Proverbs tells us again and again not to resist instruction. So keep an open mind. Devote yourself to a person who is wise and follow him or her. A fool will consume ideas like potato chips, first one and then another, barely stopping to notice the character of the one who said it or to respect the years of sacrifice and suffering condensed into a single proverb. They just swallow it as a good quote and move on, thinking these great saints belong to them. But it is much harder to submit to the authority of a person than to the authority of his or her ideas. So give yourself to the messenger, as well as to his or her truth, and you will learn the discipline of submission. Meet with him. Support him. Study her. Mind her. Obey him, sometimes when you do not agree. You may do this through books or sermons or Bible studies or consultations you arrange. Do not wait for someone to find you and to teach you wisdom. Seek it on your own. In so doing, you will exalt another above yourself.

Here is a tough one to swallow: Submit to the correction of God's people. Pride is a game of solitaire. Those who lose at it are usually surrounded by the company of good people, because wisdom is never the sole possession of one, but the collective voice of many. Here is the idea: If you want to learn wisdom, find a church and get in it. Go regularly. Settle in. Volunteer. Support and pray for the leaders. Participate in its small groups or mission teams. The tendency to leave the body that is not meeting your needs and to find one that is more interesting is, in part, due to pride. The more you are surrounded by ordinary people, with their flaws and contradictions and annoying little habits, the harder it will be for you to hold onto your pride. That is, so long as you really enter the body, participating and not just going to church to watch a sermon.

Finally, to learn wisdom, we must create little disciplines to counter our big habits of pride. But we must remember that this is the last step and not the first, so it is not the same as merely acting humble. The acts of pride are not always loud and noticeable. They are just as often quiet, subtle assumptions that we have of ourselves. So we must survey every inch of our lives for little habits made possible by big assumptions that have their hovel in pride. Then, with little disciplines, we will begin to budge those big assumptions inch by inch. In Bernard of Clairvaux's classical piece "On Humility and Pride," he gives the same advice by describing two ladders, each with twelve steps, one going up toward pride and the other going down toward humility. Each step toward humility is the negation of the opposite step toward pride. For instance, Bernard's first step toward pride is a "curiosity about what is not one's proper concern" and so the first step towards humility is "containment of one's interests." The second step toward pride is "[useless] chatter . . . about things which do not matter" and so the second step towards humility is "quiet and restrained speech," and so forth through twelve steps.[15] The point is worth noting: Pride cannot be thrown out the window. It must be coaxed down the stairs one step at a time.

If you are in the habit of wondering how you sounded or how you looked at the end of every conversation, then make a pact with yourself to never replay the videos again once the conversation has ended. If you like to debate, the next time you are in an argument you could win, don't. Walk away before you get the last word. If you like to talk, suppress your impulse to say something funny or clever the first time it pops into your mind. If you are, by nature, a name-dropper, then quote somebody famous and "forget" their name or even more, quote yourself and give the credit to someone more famous. After all, you were probably not the first to have that thought anyway. If you are an intellect, ask more questions, even if you already know the answer, for this allows someone else to get the credit for something you know. It allows them to impress you like you were hoping to impress them. If you are a person of strong convictions, apologize when you know you are wrong. It's a hard conversation to have, but if you can muster the courage to bow here, you will bring your pride to its knees.

An impeccably dressed Englishman was standing in line at the counter in another airport when a pushy, bad-tempered woman suddenly cut in front of him, slapped down her ticket, and demanded an upgrade to first class. "Excuse me, madam," said the Englishman as he picked up her ticket and handed it back to her. "First class is not a boarding pass; it is a way of life."

Not everyone can see it, but it is the wise who live in first class. It is the meek who inherit the earth (Matt. 5:5). Let us be careful then, not to be first or famous but to live right, to align ourselves with the place God has assigned us in this life. Let us do only what God has given us to do, but like the donkey on Palm Sunday, let us remember the cheers are not for us but for the one we carry on our back. Let us love wisdom and pursue it until we bear the fragrance of him who was meek and lowly.

Common Cents of Heaven

Hope in Place of *Greed*

M oney does strange things to people but none as strange as what it did to Hetty Green. This infamous "witch of Wall Street" was believed, at one time, to be both the richest and the meanest woman in the world.

Raised the "little blue-eyed angel" of Edward and Abby Robinson, Hetty got her greed and her money the old fashioned way—she inherited it. In spite of their immense wealth (which they also inherited), Hetty's parents lived as poor as church mice. They heated their home with open grate fires and ate leftovers prepared in an antiquated kitchen. They never bought something new unless the old had completely worn out. Hetty learned the trade of investing and negotiating from her father, who was so tight he once refused the offer of an expensive cigar for fear he might like it and lose his taste for cheaper brands.

So, Hetty didn't have to leave home to learn it. There are many stories of her stinginess. She never used hot water and went to bed before sundown so as not to waste money on candles. She owned one black dress, which she wore every day without washing, and never changed her underwear unless it wore out. On her twenty-first birthday, Hetty refused to light the candles on her cake, because she didn't want to waste them. But after her company insisted, she blew them out immediately so she could return them to the store for a refund. She wrote checks on scraps of paper, instead of using bank notes and traveled many miles alone to fetch a few hundred dollars she had loaned at high interest. She ate mostly fifteen-cent pies or oatmeal, which she heated on the radiator in the bank, since she never once turned the heat on at home. Speaking of home, she never owned one, but spent most of her life in run-down apartments. By her midlife, Hetty was worth over one hundred million dollars and still showed up every day at New York's Chemical and National Bank to count her money, sometimes forcing employees to stay long after hours, waiting for her to come out of the vault.

Mrs. Green spent the last years of her life the victim of multiple strokes brought on, some say, by a heated argument with another woman—perhaps the first in Hetty's life—who would not back down. She died in 1916, at the age of eighty-one, and was buried with her family in the Immanuel Church's cemetery in Bellow Falls, Massachusetts.[1]

Someone has said that the most notable characteristic of the human species is its proclivity to collect things. Told by God to subdue the earth (Gen 1:28), we try instead to own it. Only we never have, and we never will. Perhaps this is why Jesus said so much about possessions. He talked about them all the time. Howard Dayton has gone through the trouble of counting the times Jesus talked about possessions and notes, "16 out of 38 parables were concerned with how to handle money and possessions; indeed, Jesus Christ said more about money than about almost any other subject."[2] But when Jesus talked about possessions, he was interested in more than generosity because generosity does not go deep enough to the core of the problem. When Jesus talked about money, he targeted the assumptions people had about their money. He focused on the value people gave to money more than on the money itself. To Jesus, the root of our problem with money was that it displaced our trust in God with a more shallow trust in something else. Yes, Jesus had strong opinions about money, but he had more than just opinions. He had an entirely different mind. To him, money was not a symbol but a lever to get something done. It had no inherent value apart from the opportunities it could create. So, the woman who gave her last two dollars away was a legend, and the farmer who kept his things for retirement was a fool (see Luke 21:1–4; 12:16–21). With her last two dollars, the woman created opportunities for others. The farmer, safe inside his pension, had created opportunities for no one.

What Is Greed?

Throughout the Bible, greed is condemned as a vice directly opposite the virtues most becoming of Christ: love and compassion. According to Paul, those who are greedy are like adulterers, prostitutes, thieves, and drunkards (1 Cor. 6:9–10) and will not inherit the kingdom of God. That is, greed is not just a flaw. It's a covenant-breaker, and the reason, says New Testament ethicist Brian Rosner, is: "the threat that greed poses to the very survival of the Christian movement."[3] Augustine called it the poison of charity proceeding, as it does, from the love of the world.[4]

On the surface, greed is our preoccupation with material things. It's an inordinate desire to possess something in order to consume it ourselves. Rosner notes that in the Bible, greed does not necessarily involve dishonest gain. He says it is "a strong desire to acquire more and more material possessions or to possess more than other people have, all irrespective of need."[5] Rosner's distinction between the strong desire to possess and possession itself is important. Aquinas called it "an immoderate *inner hunger* for wealth."[6] In other words, greed is about the love of money and not about money itself. Poor people, like rich people, are often just as consumed with riches, maybe more so. But the ones most likely to suffer the serpent of greed are those in the middle class—those on their way out of being poor and on their way in to being rich. Rich people and poor people are not usually as greedy as those who are both rich and poor. The rise of the middle class has created new possibilities and new fears. With the possibility that we might become rich comes the fear that we might not. Forever in the middle, between the rich and the poor, the middle class is a group of people with just enough poverty to despise it and just enough riches to want more. What few riches they possess cause them to fear poverty. What little poverty they have takes the shine off their riches. If you are in the middle class, you are most susceptible to greed. Until we learn to ignore our class and that of others around us, we will always be vulnerable.

But what does greed look like? As we have been saying, each of the seven sins occurs at various levels, and this is also true with greed. As a bite, greed is the love or acquisition of things to excess. It has many forms. Here's a sample of what to look for when you're bitten:

1. *A Pre-Occupation with Money*—letting the cost of something keep you from enjoying it; taking a job or pursuing a career mostly for the money.

2. *Compulsive Spending*—buying things because you're bored or depressed or simply because it's on sale.

3. *Hoarding*—buying more of something than you need, then throwing the excess away or storing it for years.

4. *Conspicuous Consumption*—distinguishing yourself from others by what you own or can afford or being self-conscious around rich people because you're thinking mostly of their money.

5. *Miserly Living*—living without bare necessities because you won't part with the money to buy them or being stingy when you tip or tithe.

6. *Over-Spending*—owing more than 10 percent of your income on credit cards; buying more than you can afford to pay off.

7. *Improbable Risk*—sinking money in the lottery, gambling on slim-chance investments or on get-rich-quick schemes (this includes the "seed-faith" poppycock of certain televangelists).

As a serpent or nature, greed is simply materialism. It's an inordinate love of things or fear of losing them. It is never to be satisfied with our income or to be bored with what we already possess simply because we possess it. It is the tendency to assess everything according to the cost or profit. It is the stubborn refusal to let go of our money or the proclivity to measure ourselves and others according to it. It is the air of superiority or at least, the deep-seated, if quiet assumption, that our possessions somehow distinguish us from the rest of society. One may be very generous and still suffer greed if he thinks of himself as generous. Such a person proves his wealth, rather than shares it, and so buys the reputation of being generous like he buys any other commodity.

As venom, greed is our tendency to define our lives and our happiness by our possessions. What lingers in many devout people is a tendency to fear for the future, to worry our needs will not be met, or that we will run out of money before we run out of years. This is especially true among the elderly who need, not so much to be sanctified again, but to learn new habits of trust in their later years.[7] The younger have a tendency to waste things, to throw them away before they are done. For instance, the average car is owned for about three years but it lasts ten years, and so we will own three cars in the time it takes to run one of them into the ground. This is not a sin, but sometimes it stems from an unhealthy view of possessions.

And there is a price to pay for it, too. From greed, said Pope Gregory, "there springs treachery, fraud, deceit, perjury, restlessness, violence and hardness of the heart against compassion."[8] And that's just for starters. Psychologist Tim Kasser has studied the effects of materialism on the human personality and concludes that "materialistic values detract from our well-being" because these values sicken us with "a deep-rooted feeling of insecurity, they lead us to run on never-ending treadmills trying to prove our competence, they interfere with our relationships . . . [and] they diminish our personal freedom."[9] One study, cited by Kasser, shows that those who value being rich are twice as likely to have difficulty forming close friendships and more than one and a half times as likely to abuse substances, to have trouble concentrating, to fear the negative evaluation of others, and to be emotionally flat-lined.[10]

But if all these vices come from greed, where does greed come from?

Where Does Greed Come From?

In the beginning, there was God and the garden he had planted. After placing us in Eden (which in Hebrew means "delight"), God allowed us to delight ourselves in things he provided. "You are free to eat from any tree in the garden," he said (Gen 2:16). From the beginning, then, it is the nature of God to give. He seeks a relationship with those he has created and the language of that relationship is giving: "*I give you* every seed-bearing plant . . . *They will be yours*" (Gen. 1:29, emphasis added). He is always giving, whether strength or harvest or protection or rest. In the garden, we are always receiving and always giving in return, whether worship or labor or fellowship. In fact, many of the Old Testament rituals of sacrifice are, at their core, an attempt to replicate this language of giving or this symmetry between God's giving to us and our giving back to him. When someone tithes in the Old Testament, he is not just appeasing the gods or buying back his claim on the other 90 percent. He is participating in the nature of God, who is a giver. Giving is the way he and his people relate to one another. It says, in effect, "I thought of you, I love you, and I value you more than other things."

Greed interrupts this balance between receiving things from God and giving things to him in return. It plays off of our God-given capacity to work the garden and to take care of it. The pattern is familiar enough: God gives us abilities, and we use them. As we use them, he fills our lives with pleasure, and the more we use them, the more pleasure he gives. Pretty soon we begin to see the connection between using our abilities and having what we want. Where once we apprehended God through the things he gave us, greed now devours these things as we consume them for ourselves. All of a sudden, there is a separation between God and the things we enjoy. God no longer provides them; we earn them. We must get them on our own. Our work, then, is valuable only as it provides these things. We are no longer helping God to care for the garden. The garden is now the place where we earn a living, and the better living we can earn, the happier we imagine ourselves to be.

Saving Grace: Hope

This pathology of greed is important because it points to a possible cure. If greed is the result of God leaving the garden, then the cure for greed is getting God back into the garden. It is to reconnect the gifts to the giver, to shift our focus off of possessions and back onto God. The virtue most contrary to greed, then, is not charity but hope. Let me explain.

Hope, in the Bible, is not wishful thinking. Hope is "the confident expectation of good in the future and [is] almost always dependent upon the goodness of God."[11] So it is intimately connected to trust and faith.[12] Hope trusts, resting squarely on the unshakeable belief that God loves you and that he is aware of, involved in, and sovereign over everything that happens to you. When people doubt this, they grow insecure about their futures, and so they try to control them. They grasp onto things like there is no tomorrow because, for them, quite possibly, there isn't. Possessions, then, become a kind of religion by providing their owners with a temporary sense of meaning and security. We purchase happiness, transcendence, and even community. Theologian William Cavanaugh writes:

> Consumerism represents a constant dissatisfaction with particular material things themselves, a restlessness that constantly seeks to move beyond what is at hand. Although the consumer spirit delights in material things and sees them as good, the thing itself is never enough. Things and brands must be invested with mythologies, with spiritual aspirations; things come to represent freedom, status and love. Above all, they represent the aspiration to escape time and death by constantly seeking renewal in created things. Each new movement of desire promises the opportunity to start over.[13]

Paul contrasted greed and hope in his letter to the pastor of an affluent church. He wrote, "Command those who are rich in this present world not . . . to put their hope in wealth, which is so uncertain, but to put their hope in God" (1 Tim. 6:17). But look again, and note that Paul is not only contrasting hope to greed, but more precisely, hope in God to hope in wealth. Those who hope in wealth, he says, "fall into temptation and . . . into many foolish and harmful desires that plunge [them] into ruin" (6:9). Those who love money chase it. But those who seek God chase "righteousness, godliness, faith, love, endurance and gentleness" (6:11). In other words, those who seek God and those who seek riches both seek them because that is where they have put their hope. So the way to overcome greed is to shift our hope off of riches and onto God. This is a profound truth: Greed is, at the core, a misappropriation of trust. Greed is not the result of having too little or too much, though it can certainly be learned that way. It is not the result of boredom or low self-esteem, though these are certainly ideal conditions. And it does not come from living in a material world. Greed may cause these things and these things may even make greed more likely, but they are not the genesis of greed. No, the root of greed is fear or insecurity. It is a profound lack of trust in anything or in anyone beyond our selves. Harvard economist, Niall Ferguson has noted the root word for credit is *credo*, which means I believe. "Banknotes are pieces of paper that have no intrinsic worth," says Ferguson. "They are simply promises to pay . . . just like the clay tablets of Babylon, four millennia ago. 'In God we trust' it says on the back of the ten dollar bill, but the person you are trusting when you accept one of those in payment is the successor to the man on the front" (Alexander Hamilton, the first Secretary of the U.S. Treasury).[14] What people fail to understand, says Ferguson, is that "money is a matter of belief, even faith."[15] We believe the lender will pay the money back. Or we believe what we bought with the money will be worth it, will hold its value, or will provide the pleasure or benefit we imagined.

The Practice of Hope

To overcome greed, we must relearn the virtue of hope. When hope rises, God re-enters the garden and greed takes leave. But what can we do to practice hope? Here are a few disciplines that will undermine greed in all its forms and begin to restore the simplicity of hope. This will not happen overnight, but if we are consistent in the practice of these things, thank God, it will happen.

First, study your possessions, talk about them, and learn the right view of them. Many people are afraid of money and try to ignore it. They don't talk about it at home, school, or church. "The only thing I learned about money as a child," one man confessed to me, "was that it doesn't grow on trees." In fact, more than half the respondents to one survey in 2007, reported they learned "not too much" or "nothing at all" about financial issues in school.[16] The fear of money will never lessen our impulse to love it, which is why people like Hetty Green are misers. She knew how to make money and how much she made, but she did not know how to use it because she feared it as much as she loved it. So study money. Read about it. Take a course in economics. Talk to people who have a healthy view of it. Learn what it means, what it stands for, what is really happening in the exchange of money for goods.

Learn God's perspective on wealth. Christians who seek to understand their possessions will soon learn that God loves their possessions too and that he does not want us devoid of them. According to Jesus, our possessions are valuable—they are a gift from the giver—but they are most valuable only when we know their true worth. And we will only know their true worth when we look beyond them instead of at them to see what opportunities they help create. To look beyond them, we must put them into the service of God. Randy Alcorn has suggested the main reason "God prospers me is not to raise my standard of living but to raise my standard of giving."[17] Our possessions become a problem only at the point where they inhibit our capacity to trust God and to give.

Second, seek and pray for wisdom. People who hope in riches have one set of values, and people who hope in God have another. "Wisdom is simply giving to things the importance they have in reality."[18]

Some years ago, I was called to the hospital by an elderly woman named Ruby. She had been tested for cancer and her doctor, an experienced oncologist, was coming to give her some grim news. There was nothing he could do. The cancer had spread over most of Ruby's internal organs and it was growing rapidly. Rather than recommend another physician, he suggested Ruby spend the rest of her life, which he said would be only a few weeks, surrounded by her friends. But Ruby didn't have many friends. She was a miserly woman who lived by herself in a small house that was jam-packed with things. When I visited her home, I walked through a path, about two feet wide, winding from room to room in between piles of books, utensils, and clothing still in the box. In some places, stuff was literally knee-deep on either side. In the hospital on her death bed, Ruby was surrounded by her pastor and one friend, a poor, unkempt woman who came to visit her every now and then.

"Hand me my purse," said Ruby to the woman. Then, reaching into it, Ruby started cleaning things out. Just pulling them out and throwing them away. When she got to the bottom, she started pulling out rolled up twenty-dollar bills, one after the other, and held them up.

"What am I going to do with these?" she said. I just shrugged. But I had at least one idea. Then, to my utter amazement, the little old miser who never threw anything away, called her friend over and started putting it all into her hands. "Take this," she said. "You're going to need it; I'm not."

That little gesture of Ruby giving the last of her money away really rattled me. As I left the hospital, all of Ruby's money was in the possession of her friend, but the lesson of Ruby's life was mine, if only

I could keep it. On my way home, I began to pray (and I pray still) that God would not let me wait until I was dying to see what only the dying can see. That vision of a miserly old woman handing her twenty-dollar bills to someone who was poor and very confused is indelibly stamped in my mind. When I went to the hospital that day, Ruby and I had the same idea about money. But as I left, Ruby's ideas had all been changed by the news that she would soon be leaving this world and heading into another one where her possessions were not so valuable after all. Very wisely, Ruby began to empty herself of things by using them to help the few people she really cared about.

The living and the dying, I learned, have two very different views of possessions, and the dying, more often than not, have it right. To see this before you are dying is the beginning of wisdom. This is why in Proverbs, the one who chases possessions is a fool and the one who shares them is wise.[19] They are wise, not just because the Bible says so, but because in their sharing, they have assigned to money the importance it has in reality. They have done with their money what everyone does with it in heaven. They are wise, not because they are generous; rather, they are generous because they are wise, because they get it, because they see now what everyone will see later. Wisdom is heaven's common sense. Our problem is this: We were born with another common sense.

So how do we get the common sense (or cents) of heaven? We must reprogram our minds with the worldview in the Bible. More than just reading it, we must read behind it, asking ourselves, "What would possess someone to say or do that? What do they know that I still don't? What is obvious to them but is unnatural to me?" Here, in the Bible, we are introduced to characters who are very different from us, not because they lived in another time, but because they lived on another planet. These people had everything backwards. Some thought weakness was the new power, that the least were really the greatest, that suffering produced joy, and that the true measure of people was not in what they possessed but in what they gave away. Could these people be right? Does God live among the poor like among no one else? Is less really more? We must go into the Bible not as a book with a very different perspective, but as a living voice speaking through the veil of faith about another reality—a place much different from the place where we live and a place to which we are headed with unnerving speed.

After learning the right view of your possessions and seeking and praying for wisdom, realign your goals. Hope is expressed in goals. When we hope for something, we want it to happen. We try to make it happen. But people who hope in riches have one set of goals, and people who hope in God have another, even if both of them have riches. Our goals are simply what we want from life, and they flow naturally out of our values. Our trouble is that greed is a venom that attacks our values, and so it follows that greed will interfere with our goals.

It is a sad commentary on our time that most of the talk about retirement these days comes down to a number. We have reduced the idea of old age to a "bucket list" (things a consumer wants to do before he "kicks the bucket"). But do we truly believe the only thing standing between us and contentment is money? Have we ever met someone who actually believes they have enough money? And if this is true of them now, why will it be different for us when we retire?

So revisit your goals. What do you really want from life? What do you want to feel? How do you want to be known? What would you like to have done for God? To whom would you like to belong? Make a list. A few years ago, when I made mine, I listed the people and the places where I wanted my money to go if I were to die today. Then I noticed a peculiar thing: I was not sending my money there already. Did I really want it there or not? If I did, why wasn't I supporting it already? Could I expect my children to do with my possessions what

I had not already done myself? Now, as I realign my possessions so my giving reflects my goals, a remarkable transformation takes place: I begin to believe in them even more. Where my treasure goes, my heart will follow (see Matt. 6:21).

In his biography of Mother Teresa, Malcolm Muggeridge recounts how the Pope, after his ceremonial trip to India, once presented Mother Teresa with his personal motorcar. But she never took a single ride in it. As quickly as the Pope left, Mother Teresa organized a raffle with the car as the prize and raised enough money to start a new colony for lepers.[20] Why did she do it? Was she practicing self-denial? Was she laying up treasures in heaven? No, she was simply acting in accordance to the way she saw the world. She simply did not value the car the way she valued a new colony. Mother Teresa would no sooner keep that car than we would sell it. It just would not make any sense.

That was more than forty years ago. The car is rusted and gone. The colony lives on. She was wise in her investment but not because she was trying to be wise. She was only acting according to her common sense, and because her values were right, she used the bounty of her friendship with God to accomplish what God was doing.

Here is the principle, plain and simple: If you will take what you have and use it to accomplish what God is busy doing, it will feel at first like you are letting go of something precious. But if you stay with it, your hope will rise and follow your possessions into a wide open space where you will have more than you ever imagined.

What Lies Beneath

Love in Place of *Lust*

Though I have never seen the program, *Desperate Housewives* is a popular television show about a group of women from one neighborhood who suffered intolerably boring marriages. They sought intimacy with many different men, from the next-door neighbor to the lawn boy to old high-school flings. Appropriately, these women lived on Wisteria Lane. *Wisteria* is the name of a vine that grows alongside something stable, like a fence, then spreads rapidly and strangles everything else. Once it has conquered the domain, it sends forth a little white or red flower that botanists say is something like a flag the vine raises in victory.

Lust is that way.[1] It grows alongside stable things like intimacy and commitment and overruns them, spreading fast and furious. Then it sends forth a flower, not to commemorate life, but as evidence that everything underneath it is dead.

If pride is the most primal sin, lust is the most popular.[2] It is used to sell everything from trucks to toothpaste. Everything is better if it gives us more sex appeal and more time for sex. It seems like every novel, movie, and serious relationship not only includes sex, but moves swiftly and unavoidably toward sex. Today, almost one-third (29 percent) of Americans say they've had sex on a first date. On average, the American man will have twenty partners in his life-time; on average, the woman will have six. And why not? It's everywhere! Three-fourths of our television shows contain sexual content and, on average, almost seven sexual scenes per episode.[3] The epic scene, where the lovers finally undress, is a microcosm of the whole plot. And all of this seems rather odd for a culture as diverse and as educated as ours. Even if there were not better things to talk about, there are surely other things; and yet everything returns, sooner or later, to sex. C. S. Lewis likens this fascination to "a country where you could fill a theatre by simply bringing in a covered plate on the stage and then slowly lifting the cover so as to let everyone see, just before the lights went out, that it contained a mutton chop or a bit of bacon."[4] Imagine the "oohs" and "aahs" going up from the crowd as the plate is uncovered, then everyone going home that night inspired to eat. Would we not think it strange for all the attention to be paid to something as ordinary as food? Even if we left inspired to eat, would we not think it strange if the food was what drew us to the theater?

And for this pleasure we pay an enormous price. Witness the growing number of teenage girls who have had their first child but have not had their fifteenth birthday. In fact, two-thirds (65 percent) of the teenagers in America have been sexually active by the time they graduate from high school.[5] Recent studies have connected early sexual activity with other problems, such as dating violence and eating disorders, particularly the tendency among youth to equate thinness with sexiness and popularity. Accordingly, it has become common for girls to be in dieting clubs in the fifth grade.[6] Study after study reveals that sex has become part of casual friendships. And speaking of casual, researchers at the University of Texas recently surveyed over two thousand people, asking why they have sex and received 237 different answers. Somewhere on the list were those who had sex "to boost my social status" or simply because "someone dared me." One even had sex because the other "was a good dancer" or because "it seemed like good exercise."[7] These answers are disturbing because they indicate how casual—how cheap—sexuality has become in a culture inundated with lust. In others words, lust has so diminished sex that people now have it for reasons even lower than those of the Darwinists' who thought it was merely to propagate the species. For some, the "fire that is in the blood," as Shakespeare called it, has ravaged their lives, leaving them alone in their marriages. Eight percent of men and 3 percent of women, or about thirty million adults in the United States alone, suffer from a sexual addiction.[8] And the thing that has changed over the last twenty years is the people it afflicts. At one time, four out of five people were themselves once victims of sexual abuse—but no longer. According to one therapist, "there are now people struggling with sexual compulsivity who never would have been if not for the Internet."[9]

What Is Lust?

Yet in spite of all the damage, we cannot get rid of it. We pray to be forgiven, even cleansed from this lingering sin, and within hours, we are pulled back into it. Phillip Yancey writes, "Sex has enough combustive force to incinerate conscience, vows, family commitments, religious devotion and anything else in its path."[10]

As a bite, or as an act, lust is the predator within us that seeks out opportunities. It may be acted upon or kept to oneself. Unlike other deadly sins, this one is unseen even as an act. It begins in stages that are common to everyone and benign, but like wisteria, it grows quickly into patterns of behavior that strangle us. I have observed four such stages.

The first is imagination. It's the second look or the sustained image. It's lingering too long in a fleeting thought. It's walking past something and having it catch your eye and then staring at it a little longer. We imagine what another person would look like undressed or what he or she would feel like in our arms. We imagine ourselves holding or being held by someone who is not our spouse, who we do not know intimately, and to whom we have no commitment except for the sensual one we imagine in our heads. Magazine covers, advertisements, and even people who dress immodestly are always around us, and these images trigger our imaginations. We cannot avoid them. But then, our imaginations take over. We create a scenario where there wasn't one. We want more from the person than what the advertisement is selling. We want them to want us. If we are not careful here, our conversations will start to have double-meanings. There will be innuendoes and jokes and little gestures that are shared between us and them, each one suggesting something both feel but neither says.

The second stage is fantasy. This is unsolicited imagination. Now, with nothing in front of us, we imagine ourselves alone with the other person. In our minds, we make movies of us and him or her acting out our fantasies. We make that person say, start, do, and want things that stimulate us. The difference here is that the image is no longer visible. Our imagination is stimulated from within, not from without, so it is more acute. Sometimes fantasy is triggered by something that happened in the past (perhaps a pleasant conversation), but the encounter is embellished and projected into the future. The other person feels this or looks like that or suggests this, and all at once our imagination has flown into fantasy.

One step further is pornography, which is fantasy guided by images, whether in the form of movies, Websites, magazines, or romance novels. It is growing wild in the Christian world, where people believe that, as long as they don't touch, they can desire all day long and no one will get hurt. But in truth, people are hurt. The objects of our lust are denigrated to the status of slaves. Our spouses are left wondering why they are not enough. Our marriages suffer because the images we gaze at or read about are always more satisfying than the ones we come home to every night. And as long as we can get pleasure there, we have no incentive to improve our starved relationships. Pornography places us at the center of the sexual act, so we are always receiving more than we give. It burns images into our minds which later become well-worn channels. So destructive is this vine and so exclusive are its flowers that you cannot name a single individual who struggles with pornography and still has a healthy relationship with his or her spouse.

Finally, there is reenactment. This is where we act out our images. We involve others, and not only in our minds. We go into chat rooms or write letters and have verbal sex with others—even those under age. We meet them in private places. We share naked photos of ourselves. We visit massage parlors and strip clubs and gaze, and sometimes even touch, so long as we don't "buy" by actually having sex. These days, a growing number of youth engage in oral sex with their friends and do not consider this immoral. But how is this different from their parents, two-thirds of whom view pornographic movies together, as a kind of foreplay, and then reenact those images in bed?[11] In other words, they feign making love to their spouse by using images of someone who is not their spouse. Is this a form of adultery (Matt. 5:28)?

But lust is not just a visible act. Behind the bite is the serpent or the nature of lust, and is not the imagination, but an inclination of the heart that proceeds only later into a thought or act. According to Jesus and Paul, lust comes *"from within*, out of [*our*] *hearts* . . . and make[s us] 'unclean'"* (Mark 7:21, 23, emphasis added; see Prov. 6:25 as well). When lust has taken over our nature, it causes us to desire another person, not only sexually, but for ourself. It seeks to pull another person's life into ours and to siphon their energy so we can feel better about ourself. It's a manipulative and predatory hedonism: the reckless pursuit of pleasure for one's own sake.

As venom, lust preys on our proclivity to low self-esteem and creates awkwardness around members of the opposite sex. It is the tendency to romanticize ordinary encounters, not because our hearts are evil but because our self-image is so low. Even among devout Christians, lust can make us sensitive about the subject of sex. Or it can make us prudish so that even the mention of it makes us uncomfortable.

One day, two monks were standing next to a rambling brook when a beautiful woman came to the river's edge and asked if one of them would carry her over in his arms. One monk only turned his eyes to look away while the other swooped down, picked her up, and carried her across the river. Once on dry ground he set the woman down and the two monks went their way. For the next mile or so it was quiet. Neither monk said a word until the one who had looked away let his frustrations go.

"I am ashamed of you, brother. You have broken your vow. You have not only looked upon a woman, you have touched her as well."

"Are you still carrying her?" asked the other. "I put her down a mile back on the other side of the river."

Lust can cause us to hold an image we should have put down. Long ago, I noticed that it isn't the one who tells sexual jokes, but the one who can't laugh at them that has the greater problem. For the one telling the joke, it is just another joke. They tell it and move on. But for the other, it is a raw nerve, because it triggers patterns they have never quite broken. They may be delivered even of this, but it will likely not come early or all at once. Because lust plays off of purely human instincts, it is a device the tempter may use against us for years.

Where Does Lust Come From?

At the core, lust is a cry from places that are much deeper than our imagination. It touches something essential to our being, something rooted in the triune God himself. To understand how this went awry, we must go back to the garden of Eden.

In the garden, we were formed from the ground, and then we received the breath of God. The sequence is important. We were not disembodied souls waiting for a body. Rather, God made our bodies first and then he breathed our life, our soul, into them. As he did this, we were said to be made in his image, in his likeness (see Gen. 1:26). The life of God is intermingled with our bodies from the very beginning. God's image is not inside our flesh—in the form of a soul—but rather it includes our flesh, so that our flesh is as much a part of God's image as is our soul. Our bodies were created by God, and they are perfectly suited for the kind of relationship he wants to have with us. It is inseparable from our fellowship with God. He inhabits our bodies as much as we do. Our bodies are a kind of antenna through which he gains access to us, and through which we send signals to him. They are the way we apprehend God and his world. They are the means by which we express ourselves. The first couple, the first marriage, is created out of this idea. They are to know one another, to love one another, and to give themselves to one another as a reflection of the way the triune God loves within himself.

Then we ate the forbidden fruit. Interestingly, the fruit God provided and the fruit God forbade were both "pleasing to the eye" (Gen. 2:9) and "good for food" (Gen. 3:6). So how were they different? Why was one fruit provided and the other forbidden? Perhaps the difference is that in the fruit God provided, our pleasure was always in proportion to our greater relationship with God. In our pleasure, we thought of him. With our bodies, we enjoyed the world he made. But in the fruit God forbade, there was no mention of him at all (see Gen. 3:6). Our bodies, which were once used to access things God had given us, were suddenly used to grasp things he had not given us. Now our bodies were severed from their life in God. They were no longer the place where he gained access to us through our desires. Instead, we were stranded inside our bodies, severed from our souls, and alone with our desires. When this happened, we began an irresistible slide toward hedonism. Seeking independence, our bodies lost their meaning, then their proportion, and finally their virtue altogether. In the end, they hindered the very soul they were supposed to help save. Now that's a lot to consider. Let me slow the sequence down so we can look at it more carefully.

When the apostle Paul talked about people who were "separated from the life of God" (Eph. 4:18), he undoubtedly meant, among other things, that they had severed their bodies from God so that their pleasures were nothing more than the temporary satisfaction of their impulses. In fact, Paul goes on in the next verse to mention "sensuality . . . [and] every kind of impurity" as the outcome (4:19). Once our bodies are severed from God, they lose their meaning. When that happens, we minimize them and satisfy them, but we leave them behind in our quest to be spiritual. We whine about the spirit being willing and the flesh being weak. We commit sins with our bodies but honestly do not see how this affects our spiritual lives. Christian leaders will molest children; pastors will hide their pornography; church members will move in and out of new relationships celebrating each one with sex; and all the while, never comprehend how this has anything to do with their souls.

After preaching one night at a church in another state, I prayed with a middle-age man who had come to the altar to confess his problem with pornography.

"I am over fifty years old," he said, disgusted with himself, "and I have been a Christian for many years, and yet I still can't get over this sin of lust. What am I doing wrong? Is there any hope for me at all?"

Before I could answer, his own pastor, kneeling beside him, offered him the counsel one would get from the ancient philosophers. "Bob," he said, "you have to remember that you are a man—that you were born with certain desires, and these desires are sometimes strong and wild. There is nothing you can do about them, except to control them, and you are already doing that. You mustn't be so hard on yourself. You're only human."

I couldn't believe it. Bob could have gotten that advice from Aristotle. But I will never forget Bob's answer: "Pastor, if there is no room for lust in Jesus' humanity, there should be no room for it in mine."

I left the altar that night thinking we had ordained the wrong man. Even if Bob has the problem with lust, he still has a better theology of the body than does his pastor.

I do not think the pastor is just excusing Bob's sin. And I do not think he is a hypocrite. But he has a pagan's view of the body. He is leaving the body behind, like an abandoned shack, whose occupant (the soul) is staying only for the night.

Once our bodies have been separated from their meaning, they grow out of proportion to the rest of our being. Perhaps this is what

Paul meant when he described those who were separated from the life of God as "having lost all sensitivity . . . [giving] themselves over to sensuality so as to indulge in every kind of impurity, with a continual lust for more" (Eph. 4:19). This sensuality often means sexual perversion. It describes a life that is abandoned to the physical or sensual expressions. It means "excess . . . the absence of restraint, indecency [and] wantonness."[12] Once severed from their grounding, we will give more attention to our bodies because there is nothing but our bodies to give attention to. We will pamper, feed, flaunt, stimulate, and use them to gain an advantage over others. We will flock to plastic surgeons, health and fitness centers, and weight loss clinics. We will spend billions of dollars on sexual performance enhancers, skin care, and cosmetics to care for the only part of us that feels real. Lynne Luciano reports that men today spend three billion dollars annually on grooming aids, four billion dollars on exercise equipment and membership to health clubs, four hundred million dollars on hairpieces, and five hundred million dollars on cosmetic surgery (most of it on liposuction or nose jobs).[13] I am not saying these things are wrong. Indeed, if our bodies are part of our relationship with God, then we better take care of them. I only mean we pay a lot of attention (and money) to a part of our being that is already disproportionately large in our sensual culture.

Finally, once our bodies have lost their proportion, they lose their virtue. They will backfire, depriving us of things vital to our spiritual and emotional health. They will become something we have to suppress or maneuver around in order to be spiritual. "I could be such a good Christian if it were not for my body," says a young man to me on the campus of a Christian university. He says it just keeps getting in the way. He is right. His body has become, for him, the main access through which the evil crouching at the door gets in. It shames him. It ruins his relationships. He cannot see a woman without lusting for her, and it is beginning to affect the way women see him. They can see it in his eyes. They can feel there is something in the way of a normal conversation with him. He's fantasizing about them while they're talking to him, and it's giving them the creeps.

This is an ugly ending for someone who was once created to enjoy God with his body. Like the man who knelt to pray with me at the altar, he wonders, "Is there any hope for me?"

What if he were to learn his body is not at war with his spiritual life but is at the center of his spiritual life? What if he could conquer his problem with lust so his body would again be the place where he enjoyed God? But how? Where should he begin?

Saving Grace: Love

To describe lust, we began by using a vine, like wisteria, that grows alongside stable virtues and destroys them. Now to speak of love, let's use the similar analogy of a flower. Picture a plant. There is a root, a stem, and a flower. The root gives the plant stability. It draws nourishment from the soil and sends it up into the stem, and later, into the flower. Without the root, the plant will die, and yet almost no one cares about the root. No one admires it or talks about it or goes looking for it. That is, no one but the gardener who knows flowers. When he begins to worry about the flower or the stem, he knows he must do something for the root.

In between the root and the flower is the stem. In healthy plants, it grows thick and strong and sends out broad leaves that soak up the sun. It drinks in carbon dioxide and, together with the minerals that come from the root, makes the flower bloom. Unlike the root, the stem is visible and it gets noticed. But the stem is still not the part we talk about.

No, the flower is the part we like most. The root and the stem are always working, and the flower comes and goes, yet the flower gets all the attention. It is the part we hold, smell, remember, and give away. I have noticed, from my conversations with friends who own nurseries, the more educated you are about plants, the more balanced is your appreciation for all of the plant—root, stem, and flower. In other words, wise people love flowers too, but they pay as much attention to the root and the stem as they do to the flower. Foolish people like only flowers and care nothing about roots or stems. Now with this simple metaphor, let's make some observations about lust and love and their effect on our relationships.

First, in healthy relationships, intimacy, or self-giving love, is the root. It is nourished by things like sacrifice, trust, transparency, and virtue. Commitment is the stem and it is nourished by things like chemistry, personality, discipline, and restraint. The flower is sex. And what has happened to us, while we were refusing to talk about sex, is that our culture has broken the flower off the stem and severed it from the root. Sex has become an act completely separate from intimacy or commitment. It is body-to-body and not soul-to-soul. It no longer grows out of something deeper or even something previous. Sex, today, comes from nowhere and is headed nowhere. It just happens in a moment out of impulse or obligation. One woman named Ann, an art-designer for a publishing team, admitted her wantonness in an editorial where she confessed to hiring a young man solely on his sensual appearance:

> I asked him a series of questions, such as "Why are you leaving your current job?" when all I really wanted to know was, "Would you like to have sex with me against this wall here, or would you prefer the desk?" Within 20 minutes, I knew I had found my next, uh, art director. But wait! What did his portfolio

look like? I couldn't remember. I took a deep breath. If I hired him, it would be based on his looks and not his talent . . . Call me Clarence Thomas. I hired him that week.[14]

When we separate sex from intimacy and restraint, as Ann did, we make foolish decisions because we let our impulses govern us. We end up hiring people who can't do the job. We move in and out of relationships or we end up stuck in them when they don't work. We fracture our personalities. We sabotage our careers. But the real victim in this is our souls. After the thrill is gone, our souls still remember what our minds cannot.

Second, whenever we sever the flower from the plant, the flower will flourish for awhile. But just as cut flowers always die, our desire for another person will gradually diminish. The object of our lust will change. We will get bored with the same old person, doing the same old things, and move on to someone else that has caught our fancy. Why? Because, in lust we get our pleasure from the flower and not from other things that should come first, like intimacy and trust. People that lust, like the art designer in the editorial, do not imagine a long, involved conversation about their souls with the object of their lust. They do not dream up images of holding the other person's hand as they are wheeled into surgery. Yet these are the moments that nourish the flower. Sometimes a person will start with the flower by giving away sex, hoping to create the plant later. They figure that, if they give to their lover the affection that their lover seeks, their lover will give to them the intimacy they seek for themselves later. But this never works because there is not enough energy in the flower to sustain the plant so there is almost no hope for things like intimacy, trust, and commitment.

Third, the moment a relationship becomes sexual, it either celebrates the plant (relationship) or traumatizes it. It magnifies the condition of the plant, whatever that is. It exaggerates every fissure or crack in the relationship. If we do not already feel maximum trust before we are sexual, we will not just feel mistrust afterward; we will feel betrayed. If we do not already feel the other person is fully committed to us before we have sex, then later when the sex is over, we will not just wonder; we will feel paranoid. This is because sex never heals, it only intensifies. In plain language, this means there is no such thing as "sexual healing." Only fools make out before they make up.

Fourth, it is in our youth—our college and young-adult years—that we must establish the root and the stem (sacrifice, trust, commitment, and restraint) by developing patterns of behavior, and ways of treating other people that contribute to healthy relationships. The flower of sex will come later, as a celebration of the health and integrity of the stem, but we cannot celebrate what isn't there. So we must take our time establishing first things first. When I was a young man, the question we always asked was, "How far is too far? When do we cross the line sexually?" But this is the wrong question. The real question is, "Where should our relationship be, in terms of the root and the stem, before we think about enjoying the flower?" The question is, "How much intimacy should already be in place before we celebrate any of it?" Asking how far is too far assumes that the problem is boundaries. It is not. The real problem is preparation. If we move too quickly toward the flower, we are not prepared for the line we are crossing. We are not prepared for the obligations which we have put ourselves under, at least in the mind of our partner, or for the kind of commitment sex implies. This is why we restrain ourselves sexually before marriage and the reason we confine our sex only to marriage afterward. Marriage is the ultimate social expression of our obligation, trust, and commitment.

So how do we handle our problem with lust? It is not with simple chastity, as though sex was a naughty impulse to avoid, but by developing ourselves in the virtue of love.

The Practice of Love

If our sensuality is partly an unsatisfied hunger for something more than sex, then we must begin our healing by first confessing to God our failure to love and our need to know what love is. This is a tough pill to swallow. Most of us only think we know what love is because we have, at one time, fallen into it. Still, this is no guarantee that we know what it is.

In his book, *No Man Is an Island*, the Mystical writer Thomas Merton included a little chapter called, "Love Can Only Be Kept By Giving It Away." Merton writes:

> A happiness that is sought for ourselves can never be found: for a happiness that is diminished by being shared is not big enough to make us happy . . . True happiness is found in unselfish love, a love which increases in proportion as it is shared . . . Infinite sharing is the law of God's inner life. He has made the sharing of ourselves the law of our own being so that it is in loving others that we best love ourselves . . . Love not only prefers the good of another to my own, but it does not even compare the two. It has only one good—that of the beloved—which is, at the same time, my own. Love shares the good with another not by dividing it with him but by identifying itself with him so that his good becomes my own.[15]

The first time I read this I was struck by a profound sense of my lack of love. Not only did I lack this love for others, I couldn't remember even seeing it, and yet I found myself longing for it. I wanted, not only to have it for myself, but to be capable of giving it to someone else. I discovered something that day: To the degree that we lust—to exactly that degree—we still do not know what it means to truly love or to be loved. We use the word all the time but we do not know what we are saying. Good people who are married can say they love each other—and they do—but if they do not love each other like this, then they will still struggle against lust, because lust is not about sex but about love. Having sex, even in marriage, does not teach us to love. So we must begin by confessing our terrible lack of love. It is not enough to confess our impure thoughts. We must confess, in prayer, to the void that makes these thoughts possible.

We must also keep ourselves inside the Christian community. Lust is a game of solitaire. It pulls people out of community and into themselves. People who struggle with lust often distort other relationships too. But if we force ourselves to enter new circles, to make new friends, and to be with them instead of always alone, we will begin to get over ourselves. We will learn how to treat people, and this will help us later when we enter into a relationship with someone special.

And we must practice the discipline of restraint. When I began the pastorate in my present church, I followed a checkered history of sexual misconduct on the part of some of my predecessors. There were many accusations made of them. Some were true and others were not. But there was enough suspicion at the bottom of it to make my friends a little wary of what it might do to me. Just before coming, I received a message from one of them who asked, rather bluntly, "How will you protect yourself from the same besetting sin?"

"By the grace of God," I said. But my friend wanted specifics. So I wrote him the following reply, to which I have returned again and again:

I will put hedges around my life that protect me from situations that compromise my integrity.

I will not counsel members of the opposite sex in private, unless someone else can see into the room.

I will not make coarse jokes or sexual innuendos.

I will not vent any frustrations, air any deep needs, or discuss any private ambitions or life goals to women other than my wife.

I will not feed sensual desires by watching cheap-sex television or listening to humor that has a desensitizing effect on my view of sexuality.

I will not meet members of the opposite sex in a private dinner for two.

I will use my tall body to hug from a distance (or use the one-armed hug) whenever someone else initiates the hug.

I will keep my private conversations (e-mails, phone calls, text messages) with members of the opposite sex open to my wife so she has access to them all.

I will immediately deflect any praise or gratitude from women back onto God or onto their husbands—somebody besides me.

I will keep no-nonsense, cut to the heart, honest people who love me but are not impressed with me, close to my life and always in my schedule.

I will pray regularly that God will protect me from, not only an affair, but from the desire for one.

I will keep telling myself that it can happen to me and that it will except by the grace of God.

Augustine believed that we cannot live without love or joy, and for want of these, we will become addicted to lust and pleasure. Maybe he is right. Perhaps lust is the thing we do for love. The better we get at love, the worse we will get at lust, for lust is the rebellion of the flower against the root.

Lust perverts love by turning it inward upon itself. So lust and love are always opposite each other. Where one is growing the other cannot.

Just as love will sacrifice, lust will consume. As love begins with commitment, so lust begins with attraction. Love is patient, and love is kind. But lust will pick the flower even if it kills the plant. Love delights in the truth, but lust is an illusory romp with no commitment, no children, no obligations, and no hell to pay. Love is expensive, but lust is free. They move in opposite directions, these two powers, so that lust is not merely love settling for less—it is a vine that grows up to strangle any hope we have at finding true love.

An anthropologist asked a member of the Hopi Indian tribe why so many of their songs are about rain. "It is because we have so little water," said the native, but then he added, "Is that why so many of your songs are about love?"

Yes, it is. But for all who wrestle with these passions, as irresistible as they are uncertain, there is a better way. And it begins with love.

7

What the Lord Requires

Justice in Place of *Anger*

In the summer of 1870, an expedition led by Henry Washburn pushed its way through the Rocky Mountains into Yellowstone and discovered a remarkable natural phenomenon. In fact, the group found over fifty of them, and that was only one-tenth the total number found in the area.

Geysers are a sudden explosion of subterranean waters that rocket up to three hundred feet in the air, covering the earth with wet, molten ash. There are about a thousand of them in the world and nearly half are in the Yellowstone area. When Washburn's team stumbled upon them, one member wrote, "Old Faithful was the first geyser we saw throwing up a column of water [and] it was named on account of its almost constant action."[1] Every sixty to ninety minutes it lets go of another blast, each one sending eight thousand gallons of water over two hundred feet in the air.

But there are two parts to Old Faithful: the part you can see and the part you can't. And the part you can see owes its fury to the part you can't. Seven thousand feet below the surface is the plumbing—a sprawling network of massive conduits channeling whole rivers of water over a piping hot layer of bedrock that is heated by molten volcanic lava. When surface water trickles down into these caverns, the water is heated to over 265 degrees Fahrenheit and rises back to the surface in the form of steam. Once the cooler waters above have been displaced, it blows up.[2]

In recent years, social scientists have discovered another kind of geyser they call Intermittent Explosive Disorder (IED). You know it as anger. Listed as an "impulse-control disorder" in 1980, anger ranks alongside kleptomania (compulsive stealing) and trichotillomania (pulling out your own hair) as a disease you can control but from which you cannot be cured. In plain language, IED is something like losing your temper—only it's worse. It's like pulling out someone else's hair. The number of Americans who suffer from this "disease" exceeds thirty million and each one will have, on average, forty-three eruptions in their lifetime, most of which will end in violence or vandalism.[3]

Are we angrier today than we used to be? Many social scientists say yes. Like a geyser, they say, we are cool on the surface and boiling underneath. We have always had a problem with anger, but these days it seems like the threshold that separates mere frustration from mindless rage is lower and thinner than ever. On the surface, we are opposed to violence, yet we celebrate strong, often obnoxious opinions underneath. The anthropologist Peter Wood has divided the anger in our culture into two forms that he calls "old anger" and "new anger." The "old anger" was a dangerous, often forbidden zone of emotional disease. It was proof of one's lack of self-control. The angry man of the past was considered a weak-minded zealot, bereft of good judgment. But the "new anger," says Wood, is "a kind of exuberant show-off anger . . . a mix of wrath and swagger."[4] He has in mind the uncivil arguments between politicians, the loud and often violent music of gangsters, the gladiator-style machismo and bantering of talk show hosts.

> Anger has been transformed from a suspect emotion that most people struggle to keep under control, to a fashionable attitude that many strive to "get in touch with" and exhibit in public. . . . We feel entitled to *express* that emotion, and perhaps more importantly, we feel justified in *feeling* it in the first place in contexts where earlier generations would have felt ashamed . . . The anger we speak (and write, gesture, sing, growl, and shout) in both private and public now comes in many flavors: multicultural righteous, leftist sneer, right-wing snivel, patriotic rage, ironic cooler-than-thou and designer flavors like [talk-show hosts].[5]

Until we teach ourselves to handle the rivers down below—until we do something about the lava running in our veins—we will be victims of this very human emotion.

What Is Anger?

Of all deadly sins, anger has the distinction of actually being good for us, so long as we keep it pure and proportionate to other emotions. Every other vice is a perversion of some virtue (for instance, pride is a perversion of dignity and lust a perversion of love) but anger alone is both virtue and vice.

Evagrius said anger was an irritation that "makes the soul wild . . . that thickens the intellect . . . [and] darkens the mind."[6] When we're angry, "our peace of mind is torn and rent . . . [and] the soul is thrown into confusion so that it is not in harmony with itself," said Aquinas.[7] Saint John of the Cross said those who are angry think more about evening the score than they do about the grace of God. They become "easily irritated at the smallest matter and keep close watch on the sins of others with a sort of uneasy zeal, all the while setting themselves up as masters of virtue."[8]

In its most obvious form (or bite), anger looks like revenge, vandalism, temper, rage, or profanity. It's a verbal assault or a quiet withdrawal, more commonly known as the silent treatment. It is the result of fear or pain or frustration and often causes us to do unto others what we think is being done unto us. In other words, people who fear will try to impose fear onto others. Hurt people will try to hurt others, and frustrated people will try to frustrate others, often using their anger to do it. But this is only the part everyone sees. This is the anger we are told to control.

Below, a serpent lies hidden, unaffected by our confession or by our therapy, and it keeps inflicting the same bite again and again. As a serpent, anger is a state of animosity or prejudice for another person. It is bitterness or resentment or a loathing over something that has happened long ago. As long as these things lie buried in us, they will keep showing themselves in our relationships and our demeanor, in our language and our ethics, even in the way that we trust or distrust others.

But anger, in the form of venom, is even more subtle. Among the devout, anger is a contrary spirit where one plays devil's advocate to everything. Or, it's a short fuse. It's a sharp and critical vocabulary, or it's giving someone a piece of our mind. It is a judgmental, often critical view of other people. It's the persistent jesting where someone else (usually the one we're mad at) is always the butt of our jokes. It's a dogmatic mind in which we do not open ourselves to new information.

Where Does Anger Come From?

To get at the root of our problem, let's go back again to the beginning; this time not to the garden of Eden, but to the land east of Eden, to the "children of the eighth day," Cain and Abel.[9]

The first time anger is mentioned in the Bible, it does not belong to God but to Cain. The story is very well-known, and it has subtle clues to help us resolve our anger. Let's look at the story again:

> In the course of time Cain brought some of the fruits of the soil as an offering to the LORD. But Abel brought fat portions from some of the firstborn of his flock. The LORD looked with favor on Abel and his offering, but on Cain and his offering he did not look with favor. So Cain was very angry, and his face was downcast. (Gen. 4:3–5)

In spite of our theories—that Abel offered his sacrifice in faith and Cain did not—we actually know nothing of why God showed favor toward Abel and not Cain. All we know is that the two brothers brought different gifts, that God favored one and not the other, and that Cain must have perceived this as a form of injustice, for he was angry when his gift was not favored. The writer of Hebrews tells us that the difference was in Abel's faith (Heb. 11:4), though we are not told what that means. To assume Cain deliberately offered a sacrifice he knew was inferior is to infer something the text does not say. Prior to the incident, we know nothing of Cain or Abel, so we have no reason to think one was a better person than the other. After all, both came after the fall. Then why does God accept one offering and not the other? Who knows? Perhaps here is the core of Cain's anger. Perhaps Cain offered a sacrifice he thought was as good as Abel's, but God chose Abel's for reasons known only to God. God is not obligated to accept any offering. Neither is he obligated to tell us why. From this moment, perhaps God seems different than Cain imagined him to be. Perhaps God seems arbitrary, prejudiced, mean, or unfair. Both men had done their best, but God picked Abel over Cain, and so Cain was angry with God. Abel was going to pay.

It was anger that caused the world's first murder. Historically, we have put patience across from anger as the most likely cure. But our first bout with anger does not arise from a lack of patience, but from a perceived lack of justice. Abel's offering was accepted. Cain's was not, and only God knows why. The assumption that life is unfair, that God has failed; that he has picked someone else; that he is no longer punishing evil; that we are not getting our just desserts lies at the bottom of so much of our anger. Or, as the title of one best-selling book puts it, *How Come That Idiot's Rich and I'm Not?*[10]

Saving Grace: Justice

People who possess the virtue of justice may get angry or they may not, but their anger is always beside the point. They may take up a cause, like the fight for civil rights or the war against human-trafficking, but their justice is always the result of their character and never the cause itself. We have all seen people who were so engrossed in the fight for justice that they employed tactics or even adopted whole characters that were not just. Think of those who attack abortion doctors or some who oppose the expansion of the Federal government. These people are not motivated by the virtue of justice that is in them. They are motivated more by what they perceive to be injustice outside of them. There is a profound difference.

There is no better form of justice than that which was in Jesus Christ. And Jesus got angry. This is good news for people, like me, who feel things intensely. But the anger of Jesus was always tempered by his justice. His justice did not stem from what was wrong in the world but from what is right in the kingdom of God. It grew not out of his morality, impeccable as it was, but out of a clear sense of God's nature and God's vision for the world. Justice strives not only to eliminate something, but to bring something new; not only to put down, but to lift up and liberate. It wants to provide something good that has never been had by those who are oppressed. John Ortberg recently retold an incident from America's struggle for civil rights that has these same characteristics:

> Taylor Branch has [written] how in Montgomery, Alabama, in the 1950's bus drivers would accept money from African-American riders, but then would make them disembark and walk on the sidewalk to re-enter through the rear door lest they touch a white person going down the center aisle. Sometimes, for the fun of cruelty, drivers would take the money and drive off while the person was walking toward the back door, leaving them without fare or transportation. There was a sin of anger here but it was not that the black people got angry. It was that white people did not. Worse, it was that white people, who read the Bible and worshiped in church, did not rise up in fury to demand justice.[11]

When angry, justice models power and restraint. It withholds as much as it unleashes, because justice is not about feeling better once the melee is over. It is about restoring what was lost. Unbridled anger always knocks over more than it builds up, but justice is remembered later, not for what it knocked over, but for what it built up. According to the gospels, immediately following Jesus' beat-down of money-changers, "The blind and the lame came to him" (Matt. 21:14); the children sang, "Hosanna to the son of David" (Matt. 21:15); and "the people hung on his words" (Luke 19:48). In other words, while they were undoubtedly shocked by Jesus' temper, it was his teaching and his virtue that won the day. People did not avoid him, not even the children; they rushed to him even in the wake of his anger.

It seems easy to condemn all anger, even from the Scriptures with its references to turning the other cheek (see Matt. 5:39; Luke 6:29) or to the fruit of the Spirit (see Gal. 5:22). Indeed, when someone is said to be saved today, we believe him to be a more congenial person. If he is not, we start to wonder whether he is really saved. There was a time when virtue was more complex and more diverse. To be strong was as important as being gentle, to be courageous as important as being patient. There was a time for war and a time for peace, and there were different virtues appropriate to each time. A person contradicted himself, not by displaying two virtues at the same time that were dissonant with each other (as say, justice is dissonant from mercy), but by displaying one virtue all of the time that was dissonant to the time itself (as say, tolerance is dissonant from the time for war). As times changed, each called for new virtues that were dormant in the valiant heart. The wise person understood the times and reached into his character to call forth an answer. But with our emphasis on personality instead of character, all of these once complex and diverse virtues have been softened into only one that is made to apply in all situations. Now, the good person is one who calls forth the same virtue time after time. I speak of the virtue of niceness. Jesus shatters this myth by showing there is something even greater than niceness: It is justice, and every disciple ought to pursue it.

The Practice of Justice

Since it was Cain's perceived lack of justice that caused his problem with anger, the rest of his story provides some clues as to how we might learn and practice justice in our daily lives. See what

God says to Cain: "Why are you angry? Why is your face downcast? If you do what is right, will you not be accepted? But if you do not do what is right, sin is crouching at the door; it desires to have you, but you must master it" (Gen. 4:6–7).

To do what is right (Hebrew, *yatab*) means to do well, to be good and sound. It can mean to be cheerful or even content. In short, to do what is right means to do the right thing. It is not a description of one's morality. It does not mean Cain should go back and correct the mistakes in his offering. Rather, Cain is being tested. When Adam and Eve failed to meet God's expectations, he responded not with anger but with a swift and benevolent answer. He cursed the serpent and the ground but never the people who hurt him. He drove them from the garden but not until he clothed them with garments he himself had made. In other words, God was gracious toward those who, in their selfishness, did not meet his expectations. Now Cain would have the same test. He would offer his gift, only to have it rejected, and from that moment, he must choose how to act. Our trouble with anger begins when we are hurt or disappointed. Like God, we cannot decide for people how they will act; that is up to them. Like Cain, we cannot decide for God how he will act; that is up to him. The only choice we have is whether or not we will do what is right.

God is saying, "If you do what is right, you will be accepted. You will get everything you were trying to get with your anger. But you will only get it if you do what is right." Anger gives us immediate relief from whatever or whoever is hurting us. Its power deludes us into thinking we are going to get, now that we're angry, everything we had hoped for. But we are not. We will only get that through justice. Justice strives to transform things until they are consistent with the kingdom of God. Yes, justice will fight when necessary to free those who are oppressed by their enemies but never at the cost of becoming like the enemy. It is justice and not anger that works the righteousness of God.

In the second volume of his space trilogy, *Perelandra*, C. S. Lewis describes a hero named Elwin Ransom who is valiantly fighting against a villain named Weston. In one scene, the two engage in hand-to-hand combat which ends with Ransom running Weston through with a sword. As the struggle began, Lewis wrote that Ransom felt what "perhaps no good man can ever have in our world . . . a torrent of perfectly unmixed and lawful hatred" that was bent on destroying evil. But after he had finished off the villain, Ransom was overcome with a new feeling, "not with horror but with a kind of joy; the joy that comes from finding at last what hatred was made for."[12] To know what hatred was made for is the goal of righteous anger.

To do what is right involves two disciplines. First is the discipline to restrain from doing what is not right by using self-control. We must choose early to not indulge our emotion with vengeance or slander. We must train ourselves to be quick to listen and slow to speak (see James 1:19). That means we hear things and see things without commenting on them, for once we do, we start convincing ourselves to get angry. We must establish and enforce boundaries between ourselves and whatever is making us mad. By making boundaries, we agree, before the trouble starts, that we will not accept or allow certain things to happen that push our buttons. If these things start to happen, we follow a prescribed course of action before our emotions get out of control.

Establishing boundaries—and enforcing them—is an effective way of supplanting our anger with an action that will bring about a more just (or right) outcome. Think of a police officer. If all he could do was stand by the side of the road and scream at you as you sped by going twenty miles per hour over the speed limit, would you ever slow down? Probably not. But the fact that he can stop you and, without ever raising his voice, write you a two-hundred-dollar ticket is plenty of reason for you to slow down. It isn't his anger you fear;

it's the consequences. The ticket is a kind of boundary—a prescribed course of action the officer will follow in the event you cross the line. The fact that he has that boundary and is not afraid to enforce it is what keeps you driving the speed limit—at least when he's around.

If there are people who annoy you or certain situations you always find yourself in, break down that situation frame by frame and begin to put boundaries in between the annoyance and the inevitable anger that follows. If you need help, seek out a friend or a counselor and discuss the sequence with them.

The second discipline is to pursue what is right by using the proper channels. Quite often the way to justice is through the learned skill of confrontation. More than just saying what's on our mind, confrontation is the knack of engaging the person who annoys us in a meaningful conversation so that the greater good results. Whenever we confront someone, we must strive to do more than vent our anger. Unfortunately, this is where some of us get stuck. We will blurt out whatever we're feeling as though this were a virtue, and then pride ourselves for being so honest about our feelings. But unless the other person is a coward, this approach usually makes things worse and makes us even angrier.

Confrontation itself is never the problem. It succeeds as often as it fails. When confrontation doesn't work, it usually (though not always) means we have not mastered this skill. Whether or not our confrontation actually works or brings about justice, often depends on a few things that are more intangible and subliminal than whatever grievance we're trying to settle.

Picture a sliding scale, a continuum from left to right, with opposite dispositions on either side. On the one side is a list of qualities that bring a very positive spirit into our confrontation. If we begin the discussion by showing these qualities, the discussion will likely be more productive. On the other side of the continuum is a list of qualities that bring a negative spirit into our confrontation. If it appears to the other person that these qualities are present, the discussion will likely be unsuccessful.

Open Mind vs. Closed Mind
- Have I approached people to make things better or to simply be heard?
- Am I open to new information or have I settled it in my mind?
- Do I lead with good and sincere questions or with rash statements?
- How do I handle it when people push back?
- Am I collaborative or opinionated?
- Do I ever capitulate or do I just change the subject whenever someone raises a good point?

Soft Answer vs. Harsh Words
- What is my tone of voice?
- Is it quiet or is it getting louder?
- Do I listen before I speak or do I talk over people?
- Are my words gentle and calculated or are they negative and pointed?
- Have I complimented or affirmed anything in people or have I come only to voice my discontent?

Integrity vs. Duplicity
- Have I been supportive of people so far—and do they know it—or have I been too quiet when things were going well?
- What am I doing to help or to hurt?
- Have I held my tongue until now or have I told everyone else before I confronted this person?
- Do I have the interests of everyone at heart or only my own?

Constructive vs. Destructive
- Am I a peacemaker or am I disruptive?
- Am I pulling with people or apart from them?
- Am I sympathetic to the situation people are in or am I only disappointed with them?
- If they capitulate, at least a little, will people have my full support or will I take it for granted, expecting it of them, and be satisfied only for now?

Most likely we will judge ourselves as leaning more toward those qualities on the left. But the question is how we think other people will perceive us before and during the confrontation. What do they think? What vibes are they picking up? We cannot control people and there are always those people for whom any confrontation is disastrous. But the thing we must learn, before we confront, is that the way other people perceive us—even before the confrontation begins—is a crucial part of the process. Even if our motives are pure, other people will not act according to our motives but according to the way they perceive our motives. We can control some of this even now by sending forth a more genuine spirit.

To pursue the proper channels is to go to the right person, in the right spirit, seeking the right outcome. It is not enough to speak our minds.

Now once we have done what is right, we must consign the matter over to God to do what only God can do. If he chooses to honor our patience or to simply ignore it, the matter is his to decide. We can only do what is right. We get into trouble when we try to hold God hostage to our definition of justice, to say in effect, that we know what justice is and how God should act. We must surrender our right to control the actions of others and our right to assess how well God is doing.

Each of us has our bout with anger and each of us loses that bout more often than we want. Surely, your stories are more interesting than mine. But here's one from my past, when everything changed.

I learned this lesson a couple years ago when a thief broke into my car. One morning, I came out to the car and got ready to leave for a class I was teaching on the theology of holiness. That was when I noticed the back door ajar and my laptop missing. And that wasn't all. I was also short one checkbook, a couple dozen CDs, a cheap pair of sunglasses and about five dollars in loose change. I called the police and, after filing the appropriate forms, I drove off to my class on holiness. On the way, the most unholy thing occurred to me. I felt my blood get hot and thicken into lava. I imagined a thief, with complete disregard for anyone but himself, rifling through my stuff until he found exactly what he wanted and then coldly taking it. To be honest, my collection wasn't that impressive. The CDs were all forty-something music and the computer was at least three years old. But the more I thought of it, the madder I got. Over the next twenty miles, I mulled this over. By the time I stopped for a coffee, I was seething. I was imagining myself hunting down the thief and taking body parts as collateral.

I was about to erupt when I heard a voice inside me ask the question of Cain, "Why are you angry?"

"Because they took my stuff!" By now I was already talking out loud.

"But it was old stuff, and you can replace it, so why are you angry?"

"Because some little punk broke into my car, while I was asleep, and helped himself to my . . ."

"What do you want?"

"I want to catch the guy. I want to be waiting for him as he crawls out the back of my car. I want him to turn around just in time to see the beating he's about to take."

"And why do you want that?"

"Because I want it to stop! I want him to know he can't get away with it."

"But what about your stuff?"

"I don't care about my stuff! I just want to beat the snot out of that little . . ."

Now, I have been robbed seven times in my life, and each time, I was filled with the same rage. I have never known why. I always figured it was because the thief took my stuff. But here, with God's help, I was learning a different reason. In my confession that I wanted only to catch him, I discovered what was at the core of my anger.

"I am powerless," I said. And I said it out loud so I could hear myself. "Somebody took my stuff and there is nothing I can do about it. I am helpless." And it hurt to say it.

But all at once the most wonderful thing happened to me. I began to look at all of the places in my life where I was helpless, where something was wrong and I couldn't do anything about it. I remembered times where people committed little crimes, against me or against someone else, and after each memory, I said things, "I am powerless over that . . . there is nothing I can do . . . I have no control over that."

Now instead of my anger talking to me, I was talking to my anger. I began to ask it questions I never dared ask before: "Am I mad because something evil happened or because it happened to me? Do I love justice as much as I hate evil? Where, in my anger, is the fruit of the Spirit? Once I do everything I want to do, will there be anything left for God to do?"

Then the voice spoke again, "Do you trust me?"

At first I could not answer. That was the bottom for me. I did not trust God. How could I? He had let too many people get away. He needed someone to stop them. But since I was powerless, how could I? All that was left me was surrender.

"I choose to let go," I said right out loud, "I trust you. Your justice is better than mine. Whatever you decide is up to you. I will do the right thing."

All at once the fog lifted, the morning was bright and the air was clean again. By the time I arrived at the campus, the students in my theology class had heard of the incident and were already feeling sorry for me. Some prayed that I would get my stuff back and others that God would comfort me. A few of the guys offered to help "discipline" the thief if I ever caught him. But by this time, I had a better story to tell.

Since that morning, I have been robbed yet again. This time they broke into my garage and stole some power tools, then snatched the gas grill and, before leaving the yard, even bothered to dig up some bushes and steal those too. They even took the dog's leash. Good thing he wasn't on it or they might have stolen him.

The police officer who filed the report was really mad. He said he wanted to find the thieves and beat them silly.

"It's only stuff," I told him. "Besides, we're not in control of what other people do. We just have to do the right thing."

He looked at me like I was from another world.

I am.

Moderation in All Things

Temperance in Place of *Gluttony*

For six straight years, Takeru Kobayashi was a household name. He was the undisputed champion of Nathan's Hot Dog Eating Contest. It's the Super Bowl for competitive eaters, held every year in America. Kobayashi rose to fame in 2001, by consuming fifty hot dogs in only twelve minutes, doubling the previous record. Over the next six years, Kobayashi went on to set four new world titles, finishing with almost fifty-four hot dogs. Recently, he lost his title to Joey "Jaws" Chestnut who ate sixty-three hot dogs.[1]

Eating is an oversized business these days. It is the only deadly sin we embellish in the form of a sport. The International Federation of Competitive Eating hosts several events all around the world, including the infamous Glutton Bowl in which competitors eat cow brains. Kobayashi won that one too, a few years ago, by sucking down fifty-seven cow brains in fifteen minutes, making him the smartest—or the dumbest—eater in the world.[2]

Those of us who can't compete still manage to eat our weight every couple of months with the corpulent help of bulk-food distributors, over-sized meals, all-you-can-eat buffets, and microwaveable dinners. For instance, take Jim Donahue. A few years ago, the six foot two, two-hundred pound eater entered a McDonald's restaurant and, on a bet, consumed the entire menu—a hamburger, a cheeseburger, two Big Macs, a quarter-pounder, a McChicken sandwich, six nuggets, a super-sized package of fries, a salad, two apple pies, and a box of cookies—in just twenty-one minutes. A stunned manager took pictures and offered Donahue and his friend a free hot fudge sundae for the road. "I ate mine on the way back to the office," said Donahue.[3]

Gluttony is the sin of over-consumption. The Latin term means "greedy eater; to gulp down or swallow."[4] Historically, it has meant the over-consumption of food and drink but has sometimes been pushed into other areas of excess as well. A workaholic may be a glutton for his work, and a luxurious weekend at a Palm Springs hotel in California is called the "Glutton's Delight." But from Ponticus to Cassian to Pope Gregory I, gluttony has been limited to the over-indulgence of food. The glutton, says sociologist Stanford Lyman, "is absorbed in his eating, forgetful of occasion and modesty, [he is] a master of the table and a slave of what is on it."[5] The virtue most contrary to gluttony is temperance.

But I began this chapter with the story of Kobayashi to make another point: Gluttony is not obesity and temperance is not losing weight. Gluttony is not eating everything we want and temperance is not eating only what we need. After all, Kobayashi consumes over six thousand calories a day, and at five feet eight inches tall, he is still a meager 165 pounds. To the millions who only look at food and gain weight, he is the devil who mocks them.

Whenever we hear the word *gluttony*, we think of overweight people—and these days two-thirds of us are—as more or less icons for the sin of gluttony. They become targets of suspicion. Fat is out; thin is in. So the charge of gluttony is just one more reason to condescend on fat people. Most of them don't deserve it and, even if they do, our ridicule does nothing to help them. Rather, it masks our pride or anger and has more to do with our culture's obsession with outward beauty and our convoluted idea about what beauty is. Those of us who find it easy to eat everything and gain nothing ought to remember that gluttony is one sin that is hard to hide. One may lust or covet another's possessions and never get caught because his body does not bear the marks of it. His reputation remains intact. But gluttony can kill you by inches, destroying your reputation now and making you miserable until you are alive much longer than you want to be. We might do well to remember Paul's warning, "The sins of some men are obvious, reaching the place of judgment ahead of them; the sins of others trail behind them" (1 Tim. 5:24). We should not judge others lest we ourselves get judged—by the other deadly sins—at a later time.

What Is Gluttony?

As we have said, gluttony is not obesity. Nor is it the consumption of large amounts of food. To be sure, many people over-consume and, because of it, are sometimes obese. But this does not mean they are gluttons. Gluttons may be thin and fit and eat only small portions, but what all gluttons have in common is an immoderate attention to or desire for food; a continual urge to indulge oneself beyond the point of their need or limit. In fact, gluttony was first dubbed a deadly sin in the monasteries, where there was not much food to be had. Thus, Evagrius first labeled as glutton a monk who lost his concentration in the middle of the day because he was thinking about supper that evening. John Cassian was more specific, dividing the sin of eating into three sorts: eating before the proper time, gorging the belly with all kinds of food, and being always on the lookout for delicacies or what is called today "sinfully delicious."[6] Who would have guessed chocolate decadence had its beginning in a monastery?

More than over-eating (which is a problem all its own), gluttons regularly eat what they know will kill them, and they enjoy it because they value food more than their health or appearance. They eat proudly, almost in defiance of the consequences. They lose themselves in their food, throwing manners to the wind. They cannot have much of a conversation while they eat because they either gross out their company or are too engrossed in their food.

As a bite, gluttony is gorging oneself, whether all at once (like Kobayashi) or bit by bit. As far back as the sixth century, medieval writers listed five ways to practice gluttony: by eating or drinking "hastily" (eating too fast), "sumptuously" (eating expensive foods), "excessively" (eating too much), "greedily" (eating too often), and "daintily" (special ordering).[7]

Since it is hard to improve on this list (their successors never have), I've updated it a little by giving each item a name more likely to be noticed in our culture.

Super-Sizing

This is simply eating more than we need. Ours is a super-sized culture where another dollar can add another four hundred calories to a value meal. Even school lunches have increased over two hundred calories in the last fifty years. "The devil has convinced us," wrote Gerard Reed, "that gluttony is at worst a weakness which poses no eternal questions."[8] Beyond this is our tendency to hoard food. With the help of bulk-food sellers, we are able to buy six jars of something for only a smidgeon more than the price of one. What a bargain!

Grazing

Just as super-sized meals have increased our portions, snacking has increased our frequency of eating so that, by the end of the day, we consume more than we need. New companies are rising up overnight to produce high-calorie foods that can be eaten on a whim. One such company advertises "mini-bite muffins" for people who want to eat healthier, yet they package enough of the little muffs into a bag to equal over five hundred calories. Grazers will pick away until the whole bag is gone, yet convince themselves that since they have eaten only "small portions," they have not overdone it. Augustine put it well in his *Confessions*: "Sometimes excessive eating creeps upon your servant."[9]

Branding

Gregory called this "seeking more sumptuous foods."[10] By "sumptuous" he meant that we develop a taste for certain brands. We insist on one kind of cola or one kind of bottled water because we really can taste the difference. Of course we can. But when our preferences become standards—when we won't settle for less—we have sold our taste buds to the marketers. Each year, the fast-food chain McDonalds spends over one billion dollars on advertising, and a recent study by Stanford University suggests they are getting their money's worth. When researchers pre-packaged identical foods in a McDonald's wrapper and a plain wrapper, and offered them to sixty-three children between the ages of three and five, most of them said the food in the McDonald's wrapper tasted better. Even when researchers threw in a couple of entrees not normally included on the McDonald's menu—baby carrots and milk—the children consistently chose McDonalds. Victor Strasburger, who authored a policy for the American Academy of Pediatrics against such marketing to children, called it "an almost obsessional desire for a particular brand-name product."[11]

Scarfing

For Gregory this was a "ravenous desire; eating too quickly, too eagerly."[12] Aside from the sheer volume of our food, the pace at which we eat it these days is breathtaking. Rather than cook at home, a growing number of Americans (about 30 percent) eat out at least once every day. Many others depend on prepackaged meals that go straight from the freezer to the microwave to in front of the television where they are consumed in minutes. In other words, we no longer stop to eat but eat while we are doing something else, which usually means eating faster and eating more.

Special Ordering

Gregory said this meant "want[ing] foods which we . . . must more daintily prepare."[13] Translated, that means being finicky. We not only want this instead of that (which is branding), we want it a certain way. C. S. Lewis called it the "gluttony of delicacy, not of excess."[14] In *Screwtape Letters*, he wrote of a woman, the patient's mother, who was "a positive terror to hostesses; she [was] always turning from what [had] been offered her to say, with a demure little smile, 'oh please, please, all I want is a cup of tea . . . oh, this is far too much, take it away, take it away, please and bring me about a quarter of it.'"[15] She was a glutton, writes Lewis, because she wanted it just her way, just her amount; and she could not enjoy it the way it was until the servant fixed it. These days, she is just as picky but on the premise that it is healthier for her.

As a serpent or nature, gluttony is harder to detect and so it is harder to overcome. As a serpent, it is the tendency to want more, to never be satisfied. It is the lack of restraint; the refusal to tell oneself, "No!" The serpent of gluttony blinds us to what God has already provided so that we can only see the things we want—that is, what God has not yet provided. The serpent eyes what it should not have even when it is not in front of us. Like our parents in the garden, gluttony cannot even taste the fruit that comes from the other trees, because it only imagines how satisfying will be the one fruit it was denied. So gluttony is rooted in the spirit of ingratitude. The image is that of standing with our backs to the whole garden, staring into the forbidden tree, saying "More!" We are fools to believe, in a culture like ours, that we have conquered the serpent once and for all. Every interest is tyrannical, said the theologian Paul Tillich, "Every concern tries to become our ultimate concern, our god."[16]

As venom, gluttony is our proclivity to crave more from something than it was designed to give. It is the ever-present tendency to separate the gift from the giver and to enjoy it without giving thanks. Long after we are sanctified, we will strive against the bent to be ungrateful, finicky, wasteful, sloppy, ill-mannered, or inconsiderate of our company because we are too engrossed in our food. We may be devoted Christians, yet we see our lives as a feast and never see God's gracious hand behind it all. We may eat without ever tasting to see that the Lord is good (see Ps. 34:8). Or we may be saintly enough and yet continue to get out of things only the longing we brought into them. Even the most holy among us might never move beyond the level of a mere consumer (the Latin, *consume*, means to eat up completely, to finish or to waste away). The glutton may never see the grand purpose behind the meal. He may eat only to satisfy himself rather than to be replenished for something that exceeds eating.

In C. S. Lewis's *The Lion, the Witch and the Wardrobe*, this is personified in the innocent little boy, Edmund, who not only longs for more Turkish delight (the bait of the clever White Witch) but to have it all now: "Why can't we go to your house now? . . . Why not now?" he says. In the true spirit of gluttony, Edmund's taste for the deadly sweets in insatiable and demanding. He got lost in his food. He did not know, says Lewis, "that this was enchanted Turkish delight and that anyone who had once tasted it would want more of it, and would even, if they were allowed, go on eating it till they killed themselves."[17]

Where Does Gluttony Come From?

Like every other vice, gluttony begins in the garden. There, we are told,

> And the LORD God made all kinds of trees grow out of the ground—trees that were pleasing to the eye and good for food . . .
> And the LORD God commanded the man, "You are free to eat from any tree in the garden," that is, any tree but one. (Gen. 2:9, 16)

That was the deal! God had provided something that was "pleasing to the eye and good for food" (Gen. 2:9). Had God wanted, he could have made us devoid of the need for food. But as it is, we have far more taste than the animals and a wider range to our diet.

Indeed, the history of God's people is a history of feasts. In the Old Testament, even the nation's taxes paid for giant parties and potlucks. There is the Feast of Unleavened Bread, the Feast of Tabernacles, the Feast of Firstfruits, and all of the celebrations of weddings and dedications in between. Israel's deliverance from Egypt was commemorated with a Passover meal and is celebrated annually to this day.

Even in the New Testament, Jesus spent much of his time at meals and even bothered to interrupt a perfectly good sermon to serve food to five thousand people. Many of his parables were about people who threw a banquet. He commemorates his death in the form of a meal—called the Eucharist—and after his resurrection, he reveals himself to the disciples by breaking the bread, which is likely not the Eucharist, but a simple meal between friends. Later, on the shore of Galilee, it is while they are eating that Jesus tells Peter to feed his sheep (John 21:17).

But where the food is good, gluttony cannot be far away, as the garden of Eden shows us. In the beginning, Adam was conscious of God while he ate. The fruit in front of him was an extension of God's beauty, God's taste, God's provision, even God's presence. To eat was to be mindful of God, whose splendor was in the fruit. And to eat was to be reminded that God was thinking of us, feeding us, surprising us, and impressing us as lovers like to do with their beloved.

It was here, in the fruit, that was very much like the fruit God had already provided, that the devil made his offer with deceitful irony. According to him, we should eat the forbidden fruit, not because it was a generous extension of God's hand, but for reasons quite the opposite. It was a monument that mocked Adam and Eve and separated them from their creator. Far from being a taste to show the Lord was good, the forbidden fruit was evidence that perhaps he was not. If they wanted to become like God, the devil argued, they would find the secret potion in the food God forbade and not in the food God provided. How strange! But in one swift, calculated sentence, the devil separated food from its creator and in the process, subtly conferred upon food some sort of mystical power. The food would not only satisfy us, he said; it would glorify us too (see Gen. 3:1–7). The opposite was true. We ate until we were empty. Seeking more, we got less than what we were promised and even less than we had in the first place. The glory of the food was always in the Giver, and now that we doubted and sinned, only the food remained. Now, surrounded by the trees we once enjoyed, we could only eat to our heart's discontent. Food stood for nothing but its taste. Its glory came, not from the bountiful hand of its creator but from the hunger of one who craved it. Is there a more apt description of our culture's obsession with food? One of my favorite writers has said it even better:

We become convinced that these pleasures have no role in any greater success, that their qualities exist not in their placement and proportionate amounts, but in and of themselves, and everything goes off the hinges. Now these passing pleasures are forced to deal with the weight of more than they were intended to bear, to provide not only all of the most immediate pleasures but the *only* pleasure that will ever be had. Suddenly, pleasure in life is substituted for the *quality* of life and the more of it we can have, the better. What was once a passing pleasure in the context of an eternal life is now, itself, *all* of life—a haven from the meaninglessness of the absence of anything permanent. What was meant to be handled lightly, to be enjoyed and managed by its tiny proportion to the greater, higher and more everlasting pleasures is now held with a death grip.[18]

For years, the church has been silent about the sin of gluttony, referring those suspected of it to weight loss clinics and therapists. But this only reinforces the myth that gluttony is mostly about weight and overconsumption. It is much deeper than that. If the church will get over her phobia of fat, she has a message for those in the grip of gluttony. Her message is more compelling than that which comes from many of the "experts." It is the message of temperance.

Saving Grace: Temperance

Temperance, or self-control, was a big word to the early philosophers. It meant moderation or sound-mindedness. It was an umbrella term that encompassed at least two other Greek words that were more prominent—one meaning "wisdom" (*sophrosyne*) and the other meaning "inward strength" (*enkrateia*). Temperance or self-control was the inward strength to restrain our impulses. To the philosophers, it epitomized the person who was totally free. Self-controlled people knew how to act in a way that would make others admire them. But there was one glaring flaw in the philosopher's logic. It was the naïve assumption that people have the power to decide anything with total freedom. That is, they assumed we could decide to act against our passions without the passions themselves influencing that decision. They were wrong.

Today, with the help of modern science, we know our passions and desires affect every decision we make. In fact, without passions and desires, our brain is not capable of deciding anything. So even the decision to not act according to our passions and desires is, itself, affected by those very passions and desires. We now know we are not completely free.[19] So what are we to do?

The Christian view once again makes more sense in the light of our most recent research. According to the Bible, it is "the grace of God," appearing in the form of Jesus Christ, that "teaches us to say 'No' to ungodliness" (Titus 2:12). It is God's grace, coming from outside of us, that makes it possible for us to control our desires and our passions. It is the power of God's Holy Spirit, and not our own power, that rises up within us to do what is right and to resist what is wrong. It is the grace of God, acting in us every day, and to which we give ourselves that infuses us with strength enough to limit the things we would otherwise enjoy to our death. Indeed, it is God's grace together with our own diligence that transforms our appetites until they are no longer our enemies at all but the very means by which we apprehend God in this world.

The Practice of Temperance

To comprehend this grace is the first step toward temperance. This "grace . . . [that] appeared" (Titus 2:11) is none other than Jesus Christ himself. In him, the image of God in the flesh is visible for the first time. He is the humanity of God. As the theologian Karl Barth has put it, "In Jesus Christ there is no isolation of man from God or of God from man."[20] As the perfect God-man, Jesus is the revealer of both. He reveals the true nature of God and the true potential of man with God. Or as Barth puts it, "His deity encloses humanity in itself . . . It would be a false deity of a false God if in his deity his humanity did not also immediately encounter us . . . In him the fact is once for all established that God does not exist without man."[21] That is, Jesus is more than an example. He is a protégé for all humanity.

What is needed in the church today is a new and more holistic vision of holiness that incorporates the physical body into our worship of God. To many, the body just gets in the way. They cannot fit it into their version of spirituality. They give themselves to spiritual things—like worship or the study of God's Word—so they have souls that are strong and active. But they have rear ends the shape of their chairs because they have sat all day, honoring God with only their souls. With faith they can move mountains, but then they die of a heart attack while shoveling snow. They stand in the aisles of their favorite Christian bookstore feeding their minds ideas from their favorite author. But while they are doing it, they poke food into their mouths, a bag at a time, until they are forty pounds overweight. My friend, these things ought not to be.

As with lust, when we separate our bodies from their meaning, they will grow out of proportion—literally. So the first step toward self-control is to learn the place of our body in the service of God. Most of what Jesus did for us and for God while he was here, he did with his body. So what is the place of ours? We must do a little research, and read a little theology. Make a list of good questions and then, set out to answer them. How significant is it that God appeared in the flesh? What kind of flesh was it? How do things like aging, illness, fatigue, passion, or medication affect our spirituality? What does grace mean for our physical flesh? How do grace-filled people treat their bodies and why?

I know these questions sound too academic for a problem as urgent as eating. But so much of our problem is rooted in incorrect beliefs. A new appreciation for our body is not that far removed from honoring God with them. So we must learn what God intended for our bodies before we will have the inner resources to control them.

As we begin to learn about the place of our body in our spirituality, we must couple that knowledge with the second step—the practice of confession. Like most vices, gluttony thrives on denial. One study of American families found that only one-third of parents of overweight or obese children ages two to seventeen identified them as such. In Australia, only 11 percent of parents with overweight children and 37 percent of parents with obese children were aware their children had a weight problem. A British study in 2005 revealed the same pattern, only worse, with 2 percent of the parents admitting to their child's obesity. While obesity itself is not sufficient proof of gluttony, these studies prove, nevertheless, our penchant for denying the obvious.[22] This is a plus-sized problem since the journey toward any virtue begins with a stark admission that we do not already have it.

Sociologist Stanford Lyman has listed a number of ways in which we defend our excessive eating. One is to claim it was an accident, to say we did not intend to eat that much—that the food was so good, we just couldn't put it down or that we were lost in conversation and before we knew it, the whole bag was gone. Another excuse is to claim a momentary lapse of reason, the one-night binge or the reward for doing so well with our diet. A third excuse for our intemperance is the biological one. We are growing boys and girls. We have the genetics for eating. Our thyroid gland is a real underachiever. Sometimes we appeal to environmental causes. We are surrounded by people who are always eating. We were raised in a certain family or belong to a certain culture. None of these reasons are wrong. All of them factor into our sin. But they only exacerbate the problem. They are not the problem itself.[23]

The point here is that our deliverance usually begins with the stark admission that we have a problem in this area. Perhaps every one of us has an area where enough is not enough, where we seek from something more pleasure and more glory than it was designed to give. Perhaps we have a preference that has grown out of control and become a "need" or worse, a fetish. Maybe our tastes have gotten the best of us. Maybe we have lost the glory of our body inside the paradise of whatever it consumes. Perhaps we pay more attention to our appetites than to any other part of us. By the grace of God, let us have the courage to call it out. Let us name our indulgence that we may cast it out.

Another step toward temperance is the discipline of fasting coupled with the cycle of feasting. Fasting and feasting, in regular cycles, is what allowed people in the Old Testament to enjoy their food without becoming slaves to it. Feasting was the way they celebrated their bounty, and fasting was the limit they put upon their feast. They could have as much as they wanted in the feast or on holy days, but their fasting reminded them they were still responsible for their faculties. I wonder if the rhythm of feasting and fasting—of deliberately indulging our tastes and then regularly denying them—would develop in us a new control. By using such periods already in the Christian calendar (Lent), by abstaining from certain foods on certain days (as traditional Catholics did from meat on Fridays), or by devoting one day per month to fasting and prayer (as early Christians did), we could begin a discipline of self-denial that might spill over into other soft areas of our lives. In fasting, we choose the soul over the body. We nourish the invisible, eternal things already in us to counter the over-attention our culture gives to the external. More than this, we reinforce the message that the desire for something is not the legitimization of it; the feeling or the urge does not justify the action. John Cassian called fasting the first step in the pursuit of perfection.[24]

Pushing away from the practice of gluttony, we can see what some earlier saints have seen about this deadly sin, and this is the most liberating principle of all. People who practice self-control have their eyes set on things that are more compelling than their appetites. The preacher John Chrysostom said to "avoid excess on both sides, so as neither by luxury . . . nor by being sickly to be disabled *from doing what has been commanded*."[25] This is consistent with the apostle Paul who likened self-control to "say[ing] 'No' to ungodliness" (Titus 2:12) and to making our body our slave (1 Cor. 9:27). What is consistent in these definitions is first, a clear and unwavering commitment to pursue the will of God; and second, a deep and abiding resolve to bring all other things—passions and appetites included—into the wake of that pursuit. It is for want of the greater vision, for want of knowing the one thing we are here to do, that all other things become more appealing. But once the grace of God appears—once our imaginations have been arrested by the image of Jesus—we know at once why we are here and all other pursuits and pleasures are put in their context and kept in their proportion.

The truth of this principle was played out, rather comically, one afternoon in the "Big House" of Ann Arbor, Michigan, where I was watching the University of Michigan Wolverines play football. I had received a couple of free tickets and decided to take my son. Part way through the first quarter, we could not help but notice the old man and his grandson sitting in front of us wolfing down one hot dog after another, then topping each one off with ice cream and drinks. By half-time, they must have eaten enough to feed both football teams. Still, they were not finished.

But the most uproarious moment came when the little boy lifted his face out of his hot dog and asked, rather innocently, "Grandpa, how many innings are in a football game?" Grandpa just shrugged.

Who pays seventy-five dollars for a ticket to a game they do not understand? we wondered. Who wedges themselves in between one hundred thousand crazy fans, and feeds themselves portions as big as the band? Talking about the incident later, we stumbled upon an explanation: Whenever you don't understand the game, all that matters is the hot dogs! And so you eat more of them, and you pay more for each one, and you lose yourself in the temporary pursuit of pleasure because you know nothing of the game being played.

To be sure, we ate a hot dog, too, that day. But because we were there for the game—and not the hot dogs—we enjoyed them even more, and we enjoyed only one.

To know why we are here and to give ourselves to it completely will make us miss dinner every now and then. But the dinners we eat will be had with gladness and always with proportion. Then, we shall find ourselves forever at the feast of things God has created for our souls to enjoy.

More than Enough

Faith in Place of *Envy*

There is a medieval legend of Saint Martin who came upon two men, one envious and the other jealous, arguing over which of them was greatest. The good saint sought to settle the argument by framing his blessing as a catch-22.

"Make a wish and I will give you anything you ask for, providing your adversary is given twice as much."

For two hours they stared at each other without saying a word. Neither would have any blessing if it meant his rival would get even more.

"Go ahead, ask for something," the jealous man taunted, "and I will have twice the profit; in spite of your cunning, I will be twice what you seek to become." And when the jealous man put it like that, the envious man knew in an instant what he wanted. He asked to be made blind in one eye.

Envy, or "green sickness" as it is called, is wanting what someone else has or wanting them not to have it. It is a capital vice, said Aquinas, because it is rooted in pride and flowers in other vices. He mentioned five: hatred, lying, gossip, slander, and sorrow over another's good.[1] Of all the sins, envy "is the only one that gives the sinner no pleasure at all . . . thus it reveals more clearly than other sins two profound truths about the nature of *all* sin: that it removes our joy and that it is deceptive."[2]

What Is Envy?

Envy is sorrow over another's good or happiness over another's sorrow. Ranked sixth in Gregory's list, it is one of only three sins (the others being lust and greed) that consumed most of the attention among early Catholic writers.[3] Chaucer said it was the worst because it hated all other virtues.[4] Those bitten by envy have an inordinate desire to take what someone else has or to keep them from having it.[5] It's why Joseph's eleven brothers resented him (Gen. 37:11) and why the Jews handed Jesus over to Pilate (Matt. 27:18; Mark 15:10). Envy is rooting for the team that beat your team to lose in the next round of the playoffs. It's hoping the prima donna, the chosen one, makes a fool of herself as she walks across the dais. It is quietly sabotaging the young man's success as he enters the company. It is the dislike you have for people who are rich even though you have never met them. It's the skepticism a small church pastor sometimes feels for large churches. It's the satisfaction you feel whenever something goes wrong for people who have it all together.

But envy also comes as a serpent or nature. Do you have a hard time hearing someone else get praise? Are you critical of their success? Do you minimize ("It wasn't really that great!") or explain away

("Well, she had a lot of help!") another person's achievements? "I discovered a brutal truth about myself," said Gordon MacDonald, "when I suddenly realized that I rarely delighted in another person's success. In my insecurity as a young pastor I felt somehow that anyone else's success was a threat to my own."[6] The American playwright Gore Vidal put it more bluntly, "Every time a friend succeeds, I die a little."[7]

Envy preys on people who are weak and inferior, those trying to be "just as good as everybody else." It was C. S. Lewis who reminded us that no one who ever said that believed it, for those who believe it say nothing. It is only the rest, who already feel inferior, who need to be convinced.[8]

But envy, like venom, can be insidious, yet polite. It can masquerade as social justice, equal rights, or fair play. The Austrian social theorist, Helmut Schoeck, has argued that it was for envy, and not compassion, that governments of the past over-taxed their rich and confiscated their lands.[9] Others have suggested that the fear of envy is what keeps us modest. Anthropologist George Foster has charted a sequence of social behaviors employed by those who fear being the object of another's envy.[10] First they will try to conceal their possessions for as long as they can, and when this is no longer possible, they will deny it, insisting that others have no reason to envy them or that they are just like everyone else. One humorous story from the Jewish tradition makes the point:

A man must always be considerate of the feelings of his neighbors. So, for instance, if I went out to the fair and did well, sold everything at a good profit and returned with pockets full of money, I never failed to tell my neighbors that I had lost every cent and was a ruined man. Thus, I was happy and my neighbors were happy. But if, on the contrary, I had really been cleaned out at the fair, I made sure to tell my neighbors that, never since God made fairs, had there been a better one. You get my point? For thus, I was miserable and my neighbors were miserable.[11]

When denial is no longer possible, the rich will offer a token, or a symbolic sharing of their bounty. Then, when all else has failed, they will share a significant part of whatever their neighbors want. What is important is that, according to Foster, the rich are often not really generous as much as afraid. It is the fear of being envied and not the love of the poor that motivates them.[12] In other words, it is not virtue but vice, not a detachment from things but a fixation on them. It's why some fund-raisers use guilt to motivate us to give, or why some politicians over-tax the rich. Concede that there will always be envy, they say, and learn to work around it.

Where Does Envy Come From?

Think of envy as the tail end of a sequence that begins with jealousy, then evolves into competition, and finally grows into full-blown envy. Unless we have taken precautions, we are quite often in one of these stages.

Let's look at each stage. Jealousy is the desire to have what others have, simply because they have it. Jealous people have a shallow and lazy view of another person's success. They want the fruit of their hard labor without all of the hard labor. They want the romance of another person's marriage without all of the time and sacrifice that makes the romance possible. They want another's position without their responsibility; they want their reputation without their careful attention to detail or their commitment to excellence. In short, they want to reap where others have sown, to own what others have paid for, to become what they had no gumption to be until they first saw it in someone else. Jealousy is stealing virtue or possessions without actually taking them. If you find yourself saying, "That would be nice" whenever your neighbor drives by in his new car or when that soloist hits the high note without wavering for sixteen counts, I do not think you are in danger. You are just admiring them and your admiration will make you work all the harder to succeed. But if you find yourself thinking only about their gifts, without the work and the sacrifice that went into it, then you are on thin ice.

It is a small step from jealousy to competition. The seeds of comparison are already planted. Once we have learned to compare, we have subtly shifted our attention off of whatever people have and onto the people themselves. We compare not only things, but whole personalities. From here, it gets personal. It's us and them. There can be no equals. There are winners and losers and second place is first-loser. Jealousy may want what the other person has—whether his new car or her beautiful voice—but competition wants the status. And since this is no longer about their possessions, everything is a competition. Who has the nicer yard? The better grades? The best office? We even compete in the intangibles. Watch how we talk about our children's success, telling one legend upon another, until the last one talking sounds like they have given birth to the Son of God. Listen to us talk about our success in our jobs. Or listen to two brides-to-be talk about their upcoming weddings. Listen to two men talk about how long it takes them to do something. It's comical:

"How long of a drive is it?" says one.

"Well, it took me about four hours," says the other. But he has already shaved fifteen minutes off to improve his standing.

"Oh, that's not bad," says the one, but he keeps his thought to himself: "I bet I can do it in three and a half."

There is some serious one-upmanship going on. We seek to create a little jealousy among those we secretly consider our competition. And it's winner-take-all. So when competitive people lose, something more than the competition has been lost. They have lost their identity, their perceived place among the tribe, their opportunity to prove their superiority. They fear others will be unimpressed with them.

Perhaps it is this combination of jealousy and competition that creates full-fledged envy which means that envy is not something we learn right away. It comes after years of practice. Jealousy wants what the other person has, competition wants it for oneself, and envy wants for oneself what it has deprived from another. No wonder "envy rots the bones" (Prov. 14:30). Cornelius Plantinga writes:

> A truly envious person will not only resent a superior good in somebody else, but also an equal one. Thus, if he gets an A on an examination in school he'd like to be the only one. If he wins first place in the piano competition, the envier wants to win it alone. Having to share first place makes him feel like he is a loser. If he wins the Nobel Prize, thereafter each year's announcement of it makes him melancholy, for now there are other prize winners too, and their prizes are newer than his. To the truly envious person, other persons and their goods are so much underbrush that needs to be trimmed away so that one's own tall tree can stand un-obscured. We might say that the proud envier keeps running for the office of God—not the biblical God who creates and cherishes good in others, but the pantheist God who swallows all good into himself.[13]

So frightening is this evil that whenever we see it we recoil. Because envy is so dreadful to those watching, we hide it all the more. We never admit to it the way we "humbly" admit to pride. It is never in vogue like, say, lust or greed. It isn't self-evident like anger or gluttony. So we would be wise to hold our tongues and rather than squander grace by denying it, practice instead a contrary virtue like faith.

Saving Grace: Faith

Faith and envy move in opposite directions. Faith believes God will provide what we need; envy is sure it will not be enough. Faith focuses on God; envy focuses on others. Faith is secure so it can bless those who mourn; envy is insecure so it can only mourn when others are blessed. Where there is envy, faith cannot grow because our eyes are fixed upon something besides God. Envious people cannot just pray and trust, because they see themselves inside a system that is closed. To the envious, there is a limited amount of happiness or success. There is only so much to go around. Therefore, whatever happiness someone else possesses is had at the perceived expense to oneself. If the people are all paying attention to you, then they cannot be paying attention to me. If you're successful, then my success is somehow shared and is not really my own. The bread on your table is bread off of mine, or at least bread that I could have had. Envy is common among people in countries where resources are scarce or are regulated by the government.

Now if the system is closed and possessions are had only at the expense of another, then we are each on our own. There is no happiness or praise except that which we get for ourselves. And the harder we work, the higher our expectations.

We see this mentality in Jesus' parable of the workers in the vineyard (Matt. 20:1–16). The landowner hires a group of men at six o'clock in the morning, promises to pay them one hundred dollars a day, and off to work they go. At nine o'clock, he hires another group and at five o'clock, yet another. At six o'clock, the whistle blows and the day is over. The landowner calls them together and gives each man one hundred dollars for the day. Every time I read this, it bothers me, and in a moment you'll see why. Immediately, the first group cries foul and, interestingly, they do so in the tone of moral outrage: "These men . . . worked only one hour . . . and you have made them equal to us *who have borne the burden of the work and the heat of the day* (v. 12, emphasis added). Translation: "That's not fair!" To the first group, there is only so much to go around and one's share, or value, is determined by a system that is closed: the longer you work, the more you get. Hard work is not only essential but inseparable from getting what you want. One's blessing at the end of the day, then, is a way to measure how ambitious, how smart, and how persistent he or she is. Success and happiness are not really gifts but more like a return on one's investment. What is intriguing is that the first group places emphasis on their work and not on the landowner's promise. In the landowner's mind, he is obligated only to what he has promised. But in the worker's mind, the landowner is obligated to whatever the worker has earned. This is a profound difference because it creates the climate for envy. When the last group is paid the same, the first group complains, not that they themselves should receive more, but that the others should get less. If the landowner agrees, it's a double-win. The first group will not only have established their own place in the order of things, but will have kept the third group from getting too much. All of this is done in the name of justice. But as H. G. Wells has noted, "Moral indignation is jealousy with a halo."[14]

The landowner is too wise. He says justice means getting what you were promised and not what you've earned. What others get is beside the point. Doesn't the landowner have the right to determine who gets what? Isn't everything really his to do with what he pleases? Note the question he puts to the complainers: "Are you *envious* because I am generous?" (v. 15, emphasis added). He calls them out. Their problem is not injustice, but envy. And their envy arises from their trust in a system to deliver the most fair and equitable arrangement. If people work less and get paid the same, that's unfair. What is the point of working if it isn't to ensure one's earnings at the end of the day?

The landowner has a very different perspective. He knows people get paid, not according to what they have earned, but according to what they are promised. So at the end of the day, everyone walks away with an expression of the landowner's charity—some more, some less—but it is the landowner, and not the system, that determines who gets what. Those who believe in the system where everything is fair and equal are always comparing. They are always keeping score, yet they never have the same score as the landowner. When the landowner thinks things are equal ("Friend, I am not being unfair to you," v. 13), they fear that others have gotten ahead. Since they trust only the system, they will likely show up tomorrow at five o'clock.

This is how envy and faith compete. Envy believes in the system, that it is closed and stingy and that there is a limited supply. At the bottom, envy is not a desire at all, but a fear. When we envy, we fear there is not enough to go around, that we are not good enough or big enough or rich enough. Thus, envy does not spring from wanting but from weakness, from the perceived lack of whatever we feel is necessary to our comfort or dignity.

Now if envy is a fear, proceeding from a weakness, then the contrary virtue is not kindness, but faith. Faith believes in the landowner, that he is by nature generous and that whatever one has is a gift from him, so that one is free to enjoy it without clinging to it, because it is renewed every day. Today's happiness is not yesterday's, and it is not someone else's. It is ours, and it is fresh every morning. And there is more where that came from. This is why people of faith are generous, like the landowner: whatever they give away only creates more room for God to replace it with something new. Just as people of envy cannot be gracious, neither can they be grateful. They cannot enjoy things because things define them. But people of faith are grateful, without even trying, because they view their possessions differently. What do they have that they did not receive? Why should they despise what others have been given, since it is no reflection on the person's glory, but on the landowner's grace? As long as we have only what God has given, there is no point keeping score.

The Practice of Faith

When it comes to envy and faith, there is no word more powerful than that in Psalm 73:

> Surely God is good to Israel, to those who are pure in heart. But as for me, my feet had almost slipped; I nearly lost my foothold. For I envied the arrogant when I saw the prosperity of the wicked. (vv. 1–3)

In these three verses are the cause of envy and the practice of faith. The rest of the psalm is only a playing out of principles already evident here. Here is the idea: Two things are always happening at the same time—God is good to the pure in heart (v. 1), and wicked people still prosper (v. 3). Those who trust in the landowner focus on the first, while those who trust in the system focus on the second. Envy, then, is the curse of those who focus on the second. Have you ever met those to whom God was good, but they couldn't enjoy it because they kept looking at the wicked who were prospering? You would think that God's goodness and our envy would be mutually exclusive, but they are not. This is remarkable. It seems it is not enough that God is good to us so long as he is good to the wicked too. That is, people to whom God is good are imperfectly capable of envying. Why? Because even though we enjoy God's blessings, we have learned to trust the system. We have converted God's goodness into "earnings" that we receive because we are pure in heart. If God's goodness is something we get for being pure in heart, then why do the wicked get anything? One almost hears the voice of the landowner behind us: "Are you envious because I am generous?"

Behold a parable: Imagine you are driving along on the interstate highway, and you notice the left lane is moving faster. So you swing your car into the left lane and step on it. Suddenly you see a sign that says, "Lane ends, merge right!" Now what do you do? A few people immediately move over into the right lane because they don't want to get caught in a traffic jam. The truth is, if everyone did this, there really wouldn't be a traffic jam—but there wouldn't be a winner and loser either. So you stay a little longer in the left lane, thinking you can capitalize on the more timid drivers who are dropping like flies and merging. The longer you keep going in the left lane, the less traffic you have to deal with until, a half-mile later you are really flying. Now your conscience (or your spouse) gets the best of you and you start thinking that maybe you should get over. This is fine with you because you're also thinking of all the people you passed. You could have gotten over, like the wimps a half-mile back, but you were too shrewd. Besides, it has all worked out very well for you. So you find your place in the right lane, ahead of all of those losers you passed. But the moment you merge, what do you notice? All of those people who haven't merged are now flying by you on the left. They are driving like maniacs, ignoring the law and every ethic of the road. Who are those people? Don't they know their lane will soon end? What will they do then? But you know the answer. They will do what you have done. They will slow down, then inch their nose into the right lane and wait for some wimp, who is still ahead of you, to let them in. You can no longer think of all the people you have passed, because you're looking only at the people passing you. "People like that should be forced to the back of the line," you tell yourself. "They should pay a price." The longer it seems they will not, the more you are tempted to join them and try your luck in the left lane again.

This is the image of the psalmist. "God is good . . . to those who are pure in heart," he tells himself (Ps. 73:1). Then he glances out his window at the wicked who are just flying by him in the left lane, and what bothers him is not really their evil but the fact that they seemingly don't have to pay for this. The psalmist's first and last rant says nothing about their wickedness. It says they "have no struggles" (v. 4), they are "free from the burdens" (v. 5), and they are "always carefree [and] they increase in wealth" (v. 12). It's true. They can afford an easier life, a better diet, better health care, nicer vacations, and more conveniences. This is precisely the problem. They get easier, better, nicer, and more. The seeds of comparison are sown and nothing can come of it but envy.

So you putz along in the right lane, muttering to yourself, "Surely in vain have I kept my heart pure" (v. 13). You cannot enjoy your place in line because you are so taken up with theirs. That others keep passing you, even though you are playing by the rules, will make you envious, but that they keep breaking the rules without getting caught will drive you to despair. The kind of person most susceptible to envy, then, is the one playing by the rules. It's the most conservative, the meticulous person who believes the landowner may be good, but people still get what they deserve. Are you one of them? Does it seem unfair to you that others should get ahead of you when you've worked so hard just to stay even? Are you conscientious and moral, with less to show for it than those flying by you on the left? Do you find yourself secretly hoping they have an accident, that they get what they deserve? In other words, do you trust in the system or in the landowner? Is your place in line earned or is it given? That is the hard question you must face.

When this happens to me in the car, my wife will try to quiet me down but it's no use. I am too envious. Still, she will speak in gracious tones and say something like, "Why don't you take your eyes off of the people on your left and put them onto the road in front of you; then sit back and enjoy the company you have in the car."

There is no good answer to that. If I argue, the drive only gets worse. Besides, she's right. The longer I focus on those passing me, the more I insult her. The more I insult her, the more trouble I make for myself. Besides, it has become pretty good advice, coming as it does through the psalmist and translated by my wife.

Take your eyes off of the people passing you. Faith remembers that God is good even when bad people prosper, because faith does not focus on bad people. It sees our place in the line as something given or assigned by God and not as something we earn or deserve. So if others have more, faith is not insulted because it knows that even what they have has come from the landowner. If you are given to complaining, whenever someone else gets more, have you ever stopped to assess your complaints? Does the success of someone else really diminish your own? Does the fact that they are rich or beautiful make you poor and ugly? If God makes them poor, how will that make you rich? How is their failure going to make your failure less painful?

Maybe you have a minimum wage job, and all of those people flying by you are getting a rock star's wages. Maybe you work hard in school, and because it doesn't come easy for you, you get passed over for honors or the "most likely to succeed." Maybe you've served your company for years, and younger people with less experience keep leapfrogging over you. What is the thing you consider unfair? Where is the place you cry loudest for justice? Is it really justice you seek? Or are you envious because God is generous? You see, in the end, our problem with envy is really our problem with God. We don't like the way he distributes success or beauty or happiness. And our problem with God is exactly that—our problem. There is no other way to deal with this except to take our eyes off of whatever he has given to others, and put them onto whatever he has given to us. That's the second part.

Put them onto the road in front of you. Driving through Chicago one summer, my friend Don noticed a driver on his left trying to merge in front of him. Already having given up his space many times, Don refused to let the man in. A quarter-mile later they were still jostling—the driver trying to squeeze in and Don riding the bumper of the car in front of him. Suddenly Don, now obsessed with the driver on his left, plowed into the driver in front. That's what happened to the psalmist too. When he envied the arrogant, his envy nearly destroyed him. He was "punished every morning" (v. 14) by the success of the people he despised. The more galling his enemies were, the more sour his own spirit became. In the end, there is not much difference between those who "speak with malice" (v. 8) as the wicked do, and those who hold them in contempt.

When we put our eyes back on the road, we handle our business. We meet our obligations at the office, in class, to our family, or on the team. We work conscientiously. We choose wisely. We do the right thing. When people envy, they become lax in their performance because they are obsessed more with reward than performance. So we have to consciously, and outwardly, promise to use whatever God has given us to do whatever is in front of us.

Enjoy the company you have in the car. "I am always with you [God]," says the psalmist after he has come to his senses. "You hold me by my right hand. You guide me with your counsel . . . Whom have I in heaven but you? And earth has nothing I desire besides you"

(vv. 23–25). These are pretty strong words. And notice the difference in his attitude. I counted seventeen references to "them," and only one to "God," at the beginning of the psalmist's rant (vv. 4–12). No wonder he envied people. But in the second half of the psalm (vv. 18–27), the ratio is almost the exact opposite: sixteen references to God (or "you") and only four to the people passing by. This shift, from what others have to what we have, from what we have earned to what we've been given is the discipline of gratitude. More than any other discipline, gratitude will displace the vice of envy. Envy stands on the shoulders of all we have and eyes all we want. But faith gets on its knees and looks up to all we have—and wants nothing.

Gratitude is a learned behavior, and it is not related to our circumstances. No amount of favor will make us more grateful if we are not already that way, because gratitude is a character and the lack of gratitude a character flaw. And you cannot be rid of a character flaw by throwing more things at it. Gratitude does not just happen to people once they grow up or get more stuff. We must learn it now—wherever we are—or forever be done with the childish notion that we will learn it later.

The sin of envy creeps around every blessing and threatens to turn each into a score. It sours what we were given into something that we earned and makes us proud of ourselves and less grateful to God. But in every envious heart is the voice of a generous landowner asking us to trust him and his distribution of things. "What is that to you?" he says. "You must follow me." The faith to counter envy, then, is not a fragile conviction that things will all come out square in the end. Faith is a deep and rooted confidence in the landowner himself. It is a willingness to accept whatever he has dealt us because it is him that we desire. It asks us daily to hold up what little we have—as Jesus held up a little boy's lunch—and pronounce a blessing over it, saying, "It is enough!"

Father, it is more than enough.

10

A Road Less Taken

Courage in Place of *Sloth*

In his book, *Living on the Ragged Edge*, Charles Swindoll tells a funny story about his friend who taught high school just long enough to know he shouldn't be teaching high school. One year, he was assigned to teach a rather dreary subject to an even drearier group of students. The teacher fumbled through his first lecture, but the students paid no attention. Finally, when he had reached his breaking point, he whirled around and began to write in large letters across the board: A-P-A-T-H-Y! He then underlined it twice.

> One of the dull students up front frowned as he struggled to read the word. Unable to pronounce it, he tilted his head to one side as he started spelling it aloud, "A-P-A-T-H-Y." He mispronounced it, "Aa-payth-ee," then he leaned over and muttered to his buddy, "What in the world is 'a-paythee'?" His friend yawned back with a sigh, "Who cares?"[1]

"Who cares?" or sloth, is the last sin on our list, though some in the early church put it first for the same reason: The sin of sloth, or the virtue of courage, underscores every other sin and virtue, making them easier.

"There are times," wrote Dorothy Sayers, "when one is tempted to say that the great sprawling, lethargic sin of Sloth is the oldest and the greatest of the sins and the parent of all the rest."[2] Why? If we are lazy, or if we shrink back from trouble, then every other sin will have a heyday. For a life without discipline will run to weeds as quickly as a garden; only a life is much harder to take back. If we are strong, courageous, and disciplined, we will fight through this life with valor, and every other sin will diminish while every other virtue will multiply. Simply put, those who are harder on themselves will find life a little easier. Those who are easy on themselves will find life insufferable.

What Is Sloth?

But what exactly is sloth? What could it possibly have to do with us? Aren't we overworked? Actually, the meaning of sloth has evolved over the years, from something far different to something more like laziness today.

In the Bible, sloth is a kind of slowness that is always opposite a virtue called vigilance. The meaning of sloth evolves according to how each generation defines vigilance.

To the desert monks, sloth was mental dullness, the failure to fix the mind on higher things or to keep it busy. Evagrius called it the noonday demon and said it was the most oppressive of all. Sloth made the sun move slowly and the day seem fifty hours long. It tempted the good monk to look out his window and dream of being somewhere else. Then, before long, he would dream of supper. Sloth caused him to relax in his disciplines or even abandon them altogether.[3] When afflicted, the monk would run through his rituals without engaging in them, like what some people do in church today.

Two centuries later, Gregory defined vigilance as discipline and valor, so sloth was an aversion to hard things. It was taking the easy way out, to wrap oneself in trivial pursuits. Sloth, said Gregory, "braces itself not toward higher things [but] lets itself run loose, uncared for in lower desires."[4] Because it would not pursue great things, sloth is too easily entangled in small things and often at the behest of someone else. The journalist Henry Fairlie called it the "hatred of all spiritual things which entail effort."[5]

Still later, Aquinas thought vigilance was the ability to perform religious duties, and so sloth was a lack of appetite for God; a coolness for our first love. It was "sadness concerning a spiritual and internal good. As such, "it suppresses spiritual passion so that it does not rise to act."[6] In other words, sloth is too-easily satisfied with one's spirituality. The mystic, St. John of the Cross said it "runs fretfully away from everything that is hard . . . the more spiritual a thing is, the more frustrating they find it."[7] Twentieth-century mystic, A. W. Tozer criticized those who were too easily satisfied by the progress of their faith. He writes:

> One of the great foes of the Christian is religious complacency. The man who believes he has arrived will not go any further; from his standpoint it would be foolish to do so . . . The present neat habit of quoting a text to prove we have arrived may be a dangerous one if in truth we have no actual inward experience of the text. Truth that is not experienced is no better than error, and may be fully as dangerous.[8]

Siding with Aquinas, the contemporary Catholic writer, Peter Kreeft, argues there are two kinds of sloth: (1) refusing to work on earthly tasks and (2) refusing to work on heavenly tasks. He says the latter is a mortal sin, because it does not allow us to even seek God, which means we will never find him.[9] The slothful may be either lazy or busy, they may sleep or fidget, run the remote or run their mouth, but their preoccupation with trivial things prohibits them from pursuing the all-consuming God with a sustained eye.

Today, after the rise of agriculture and industry in our nation, vigilance has come to mean hard work and so sloth is weakness or low ambition. It's the failure to produce. It's a poor work ethic typified by the proverbial "couch potato" or the sleep-until-noon adolescent. This idea of sloth has found great support in Proverbs with the mention of the sluggard who "is slack in his work" (Prov. 18:9).

So the meaning of sloth has evolved over time, and yet there is still a locus, a point where all of these definitions intersect. Sloth, or *acedia* as it was once called, is simply weakness or weariness. It is a disinclination to act—to be sluggish or slow—and we may show it mentally when we lack either depth or certainty. We may show it spiritually when we lack joy or intensity. We may show it physically when we lack energy or ambition. We may even show it socially when we lack patience or refuse to put forth the effort to be with others.

As a bite, sloth takes the easy way out. It sleeps too long and can't get going in the morning. It lives by clichés. It talks slow and thinks even slower. It shows up for work and then avoids it like the plague. Sloth has many forms.

Sloth loafs. We have all met people who have a knack for getting other people to do their work, for doing as little as possible, and for creating whole systems that save themselves work, so they can piddle for hours at things that will not matter a whit in the hour of their death. Sloth does not value labor but only the fruit of labor, and so any fruit that can be had without labor is the only fruit sloth enjoys.

Sloth procrastinates. It does not make the call or schedule the appointment or get started on the job because it dreads all that one is in for. Gregory warned, "When we will not do at the right time what we can, before long, when we will, we cannot."[10] Derek Kidner observed, "The slothful person does not commit himself to refuse anything but he deceives himself by the smallness of his surrenders; so by inches and by minutes the opportunity slips away."[11]

Sloth daydreams. It imagines itself to be done with something that one has not even started. "Pastor, I can't decide what I want to be and I want your help," said the lanky, lazy sixteen-year-old, leaning over my desk. "Do you think God wants me to be a cardiologist or a neurologist?" Knowing the boy, I knew immediately what God wanted. "I think he wants you to finish high school," I said. That was twenty years ago and he still hasn't. Sloth will let us dream big dreams because, in the end, our lives never take the shape of our dreams anyway, but of our disciplines and our decisions.

Sloth fritters. One of its tricks, says Dorothy Sayers, "is to dissemble itself under the cover of whiffling activity of body [so that] we think that if we are busily rushing about and doing things, we cannot possibly be suffering from sloth."[12] But in fact, the easily distracted busybody or the workaholic is just as likely to be slothful, not because he won't work but because he can't decide. This is what Gregory meant when he said they do not pursue great things so they are too easily entangled in small things and often at the behest of someone else. C. S. Lewis noted that lazy people are the only ones who work too hard. They have deferred the hard interior work of knowing what it is they were called to do over to someone else, so they spend their whole lives working for someone else's dreams or cleaning up someone else's mess. They cannot say no to someone else's idea, precisely because they have not bothered to first say yes to their own. "It is not that the slothful are inactive," notes Ken Bazyn, "but that the tasks they perform seem so second-rate."[13] He describes a character who has "never smelled a flower, never looked at a star, never loved anyone, indeed has never done anything in his life except add up figures . . . and all day he says to himself, 'I am busy with things that matter,' but in the end, they do not matter as much as the things he ignored to do them."[14]

Finally, as a bite, sloth quits. When the rich fool plotted his retirement, he said he would build larger barns and then say to himself, "you have plenty of good things laid up for many years. *Take life easy*; eat, drink and be merry" (Luke 12:19, emphasis added). Not long ago, I discovered an ugly idol in my life called "And then I'll be done!" Whenever I was in the middle of something hard, I imagined the day when it would all be over and I would be done. I will have earned the degree, finished the manuscript, completed the project, fixed the problem, served my time, and in the twilight of my life, I will be done! There will be nothing more to do except enjoy the fruit of my labor. Then I can just sit down or go outside to play. It occurred to me that I valued rest more than labor, and that's why I look forward to being done. From my childhood, I could not wait for the school year to end or even for the day to be over. Now, I was deferring it all to retirement—the great weekend at the end of life that stretches into an eternal vacation in the life after.

As a serpent, sloth is more subtle. It is a creeping sadness of the soul. It is a faintheartedness, a moral weakness or timidity. When Jeremiah pronounced "A curse on him who keeps his sword from bloodshed" in the heat of battle, he surely had this in mind (see Jer. 48:10). In some, there is an unwillingness to commit or to confront, to get themselves dirty or bloody in battle. As a serpent, sloth may take the form of fear ("I might get hurt") or fatigue ("I am too tired") or failure ("I tried that once"). It is silence when an argument is necessary. It is complacency when others need a voice. Dorothy Sayers said sloth is called "tolerance" in this world, but in hell it is called "despair." She writes, "It is a sin which believes in nothing, cares for nothing, seeks to know nothing, interferes with nothing, enjoys nothing, loves nothing and only remains alive because there is nothing it would die for."[15] Surely this is worse than the mere bite of sloth. This is a preoccupation with oneself and one's agenda or the lack thereof. Just as this type of sloth is deeper and more serious than the idle thoughts of a monk in the middle of the day, so the cleansing from this kind of sloth is possible only through the work of the Holy Spirit.

But even more insidious than the bite or the serpent is the venom of sloth, the part that lingers even after the sin is forgiven and the nature cleansed. The venom gives us trouble for years, affecting the way we function. It weakens us and diminishes our glory and health. As venom, sloth is cowardice, a hesitating spirit, and an interior weakness. It will make us soft and easily intimidated. It will make us impatient or frustrated. This lack of courage does not come upon us all at once but subtly and slowly. It introduces itself as a way out, as relief or shade or a much-needed break. It looks at whatever we have done and calls it "good enough for now." It points to those already done for the day. It tells us to be safe, to quit while we're ahead, and to wait for a better time. I wonder if every person carries within the seeds of sloth which are suppressed—even after sanctification—for we have all met people who are pure in heart but weak and afraid.

Where Does Sloth Come From?

As we have all along, let's go back to the garden of Eden to learn where our trouble began. "In the beginning God created . . . [and] on the seventh day he rested from all his work" (Gen. 1:1; 2:2). Thus God works before he rests. In the creation story, all work is moving steadily toward a culmination of rest, not fatigue or burnout, not a vacation or a break but rest, the stoppage of activity, the cessation of all things. The Sabbath, then, is not the end of work but the beginning of rest. It is the day of God's delight—a day when everything is as it should be. The Jews taught us that the first week did not climax with the creation of man but rather ended with the Sabbath. It was the reset button at the end of each week—the day toward which everything moved and for which everything longed. The seventh day, and not the sixth, was God's magnum opus. On the seventh day, God and humanity would enjoy the things they had grown together all week. God would stroll freely in and out among us, as he did in the garden, in the cool of the day.

Sloth plays off of this natural desire for Sabbath, though not as a complement to our work but as its competition. In the end, sloth destroys even the Sabbath it seeks because our rest is only sweet so long as it comes at the end of our work. Where there is no work, there is no real rest. "There is no pleasure in having nothing to do," wrote the American writer, Mary Little. "The fun is in having lots to do and *not* doing it."[16] That is one difference between sloth and rest. The slothful quite often have nothing to do because they have long ago quit. They have never taken up a task or gotten involved in a struggle that did not introduce itself to them. They walked away from their obligations the moment things got hard. But those who rest cease from their labors long enough to enjoy them, then return tomorrow to the work that brings them dignity.

That is the way it's supposed to be. We are to subdue the earth and as we do, he will "give [us] every seed-bearing plant" (Gen. 1:28–29). We are to work the garden and he will give us every tree (2:15–16). The slothful have this backwards. They want to eat where they have not planted, rest where they have not worked, consume what they have not produced, spend what they have not earned, conquer when they have not fought, and be honored when they have not sacrificed. They want, in fact, a Sabbath without something to do.

Saving Grace: Courage

The slothful hope that life will be easy, or at least more fun. Whenever it isn't, they are quickly distracted or afraid, and they lose heart. Weariness and weakness set in, and to counter them, we must develop the virtue of courage. But courage is more than hanging on. Courage is tenacity at noonday—dependability, maturity, vitality, sturdiness of the soul. When people lack courage, they will cave in. They will act with duplicity. They will turn their attention toward preserving whatever situation gives them the least amount of trouble. Afraid of being criticized, they will throw every other virtue to the wind. They lack guts, bravery, stamina, and boldness. So they are frail or flimsy. Sometimes people who lack courage still sin, even though they are mostly good at heart, just because they are weak.

What do you do—or fail to do—because you lack courage? What might you be, if only it were easier? From what possibilities do your fears keep you? To such people, the writer of Hebrews addresses a fiery letter that seeks to inspire them to come back to the battle they abandoned. He tells them to "run with perseverance the race that is marked out for us . . . [and to] endure hardship as discipline [for] God is treating [us] as sons" (Heb. 12:1, 7). To the weak, he says life is not a feast but a predicament. It is the first thing the slothful forget, and until they make this fundamental change in their expectations, all other attempts to motivate them will fail because, in the end, the slothful are not lazy; they are weak. Pleasure is their crowning virtue. Hardship means something is wrong. Every pursuit—whether religion, education, relationships, work, even duty—is assessed by whether or not it was easy or fun. The trouble is that they can never succeed in making all ventures easy, and so, when they confront what they cannot make easy, they quit. They shrink back. To these people, the preacher of Hebrews is clear: "Life is a predicament; show courage!" But how?

The Practice of Courage

First, choose your heroes. The preacher of Hebrews tells us we are surrounded by a "cloud of witnesses" who have marked out the race for us (Heb. 12:1). Scholars tell us the race marked out is the long and bloody line of martyrs who gave up, not only comfort, but their very lives for the sake of Christ. Or it is Christ himself who endured the cross for the joy directly behind it (12:2). To gain courage, we must choose models from Christianity's past and use them as our cloud of witnesses. I have around me photographs of A. W. Tozer, C. S. Lewis, Thomas Merton, Charles Spurgeon, Pope John Paul II, Dietrich Bonhoeffer, and a few others. These are my witnesses. I also have a few that are still alive. Whenever I tire or get hurt or get caught in minutia, I look at them and wonder, did they ever have days like this? What did they have to endure? And how did they do it?

Once we find them, we must throw off the things that entangle us. These are not sins but habits that distract us. There is nothing wrong with them except that they get in the way. John Wesley noted people in his day that had certain luxuries and were "constantly the parent of sloth . . . the more of meat and drink [they] devour the less taste [they] will have for labor."[17] For us, it might be technology. Maybe we spend too much time chasing it and repairing it for those few hours when it will serve us. For others, it might be television. For some it will be hobbies, or food, or useless chatter. The important thing is that, with the help of our witnesses, our cloud of heroes, we choose the destiny we wish to have. We must periodically recalibrate, strengthen, or straighten up.

Second, take a Sabbath. Just as gluttony may overtake someone who, of all things, never allows himself to feast, so sloth may creep upon someone who never allows himself to rest. I wonder if some of our apathy is really the rent coming due on long periods of time without a regular Sabbath. In truth, we are not wired to work and produce all of the time. Just as work precedes the Sabbath, a Sabbath must follow the work. What appears to be apathy or daydreaming might be only the body or the mind getting its time off whether we like it or not. The "take ease" retirement that many in their fifties look forward to might be a muffled cry for a Sabbath deferred to the end of life. But a Sabbath is not a day off. Rather, it is the sanctification of time and of work. It is when our souls finally catch up with our bodies. In her book, *Keeping the Sabbath Wholly*, Marva Dawn says there are four disciplines to practicing it: (1) Resting—where we ponder and reflect on God's grace, recounting the ways he has kept his promises; (2) Ceasing—where we stop our activity and get in touch with our mortality, we review our agendas and eliminate things from our schedule; (3) Feasting—where we enjoy the company of family and friends over a meal and recommit ourselves to the community; and (4) Embracing—where we reevaluate our vocation and ponder what new ventures God might be calling us into.[18] A good community is essential in all of these as none of them are to be practiced alone.

Third, pay attention to the little things that are controlling you. Things come apart. Vision blurs. Ideals settle into routines. Dreams get dismembered by a thousand interruptions. Modern technology has only enhanced the ways for these interruptions to get into our lives. Perhaps somewhere in your life there is a voice mail, an e-mail, a text message, or something else waiting for you, and if you are not careful, you will spend your whole day answering someone else's questions and following someone else's idea. Details will leave you with only a hollow satisfaction that you are current in the news or caught up in your work, but they will never in themselves produce something significant that you can leave behind. You must do that in addition to the details. Still, there must be a time to take care of the little things or they will mount up and drain away energy reserved for the big things. To refocus, one small business schedules a day each month they call

"Eat that Frog," named after Brian Tracy's book on procrastination.[19] They require their employees to submit a list of all the little, petty things they have put off and hate doing or to resurrect one project they have failed to finish and to spend an entire Friday completing them. It is the most dreaded day of the month—like eating a frog, they say. But according to one employee, it's the most productive day, in terms of the company's vision, because it gets little things out of the way and frees employees to get back to their main task.

Finally, be strong and courageous! It seems there is a moment when sloth is first introduced, and even voted upon. Then it rules the day. For each person, that moment is different. For some, it comes right after the initial desire. They imagine themselves to have already done what they have not even started. To them the Spirit says, "Press on!" For another, it comes with the first stiff wind of resistance. They want never to make an enemy; they want to be liked by everyone all of the time. To them the Spirit says, "Be strong!" For someone else, sloth is introduced the moment they confront pain or an unexpected loss. Things go wrong, they take more time and money than we thought. Maybe it just "wasn't meant to be." To them the Spirit says, "Endure hardship!" Still, for someone else, sloth comes as the moment they are called away, or distracted. More work is added to their list and they never get back to what they were doing. In this moment, they must press on.

Those who watch movies today know of a little feature that has been added to the formatted versions they can watch at home. One feature is called the "alternative ending." It doesn't change any of the characters or the scenes, but the ending is different, and when it is, sometimes even the plot has changed. Recently, we watched one in our house and we were amazed at the impact of the last five minutes had upon the rest of the movie. Yes, how the movie ends changes the way we watch it. Now imagine a movie that begins and proceeds in exactly the same order, but in the last five minutes, you discover things in the alternative ending that make you want to go back and watch the movie again, because now you will be looking for an entirely different set of actions. You will hear things in the dialogue you ignored the first time. You will notice the cameo appearance of certain characters that didn't mean anything before. Even the silence will tell you something. You will watch it saying, "Of course, of course . . . how did I miss that?" because it's all in the way the movie ends.

My friend, there is an alternative ending to this life. There is the one everyone else expects, but there is another one as well. In this ending, God himself restores you. He makes you strong and steadfast. Once you see it, your courage rises. You see, in the same situations, things you missed before. Once meaningless conversations, those appointments you dread keeping, the people you avoid, the little compromises you make when no is looking, even the times when God is silent have a new gravity that weighs heavy on your soul. The power of the alternative ending lands you, happily ever after, right in the place you hoped for. But it also reinterprets every situation you are in today.

Perhaps there is no greater need in our soft generation than the need for courage. Those who possess it are rare indeed and will be seen by their contemporaries as an object peculiar and even frustrating. As yeast, they seem foreign to the culture they make rise. They do not laugh as their culture laughs or accept what their culture assumes. They follow a voice that is beyond all other voices, and with humility, follow it wherever they must—no matter what. While others adjust to their society, these never tire of getting their society to adjust to them. They are the heroes in the twilight of our civilization.

Back to Eden

In Which We Fell

Throughout our study, we have seen that good and evil—virtue and vice—are always present, sometimes dormant but always at war. Though there are some that are as given over to evil as others are given to good, both powers compete for space in our souls. Those in one of them will be always tempted by the other. The way to be whole is through overcoming evil with good, by cooperating with the Holy Spirit and his work in our lives.

But the matter of overcoming evil is not a simple process, because evil plays on things that are often out of our control—things like desires, emotions, relationships, circumstances, limitations, cultural biases, and so forth—and before we can stop ourselves, we are stuck with a habit we do not want. Hence, "the evil [we] do not want to do—this [we] keep on doing" (Rom. 7:19). To be told we only need to "get right with God" or to be "sanctified" or to discipline ourselves in the face of such resourceful enemies only leaves us feeling defeated and powerless. We cannot take this for long. After we have struggled for years, without victory over sin, we will usually fall into one of two patterns. You have likely seen them both.

One is the feeling we are not truly forgiven, that we are still cross-ways with God. This always produces other feelings of guilt, fear, apathy, or depression. As a result, many recommit themselves to Christ again and again, not for love but fear. I am thinking of the young man who appeared before our ordination board some years ago, and told how he was "born again" three times. I nearly fell off my chair. Really? Born again three times? Isn't that more like reincarnation? What the young man was saying was that the first two didn't take. They didn't have the effect on him he was hoping for, so he quit and later, when he could stand it no longer, he committed himself again. These people mean well. They're not faking. But all of their resolve is no match for the hard and persistent problem of sin. One young man told me he used to be a Christian but decided it was too hard for him, so he quit. "At least I'm not a hypocrite," he said.

Another pattern we fall into is living a divided life. With our sins still clinging to us, we learn to live out of two rooms, one in which we are Christians and the other in which we are just ordinary folk. Each room has its own set of aspirations. Each has its own ethics, its own obligations, and its own audience we play to. We do not think of spiritual things while we are in the other room, and we do not think of our jobs or of our families while we are in the spiritual room. We do this, not because we are hypocrites, but because we cannot live with the frustration of doing evil while we are trying to be good.

So the question is not whether or not we will fail. We will. The question is what happens next. We began this book by asking, "Are the holy among us still sick?" Now, let us turn the question around: "Can the sick among us still be holy?"

What Happens When We Blow It?

Fred Merkle played sixteen years of professional baseball, most of them with the New York Giants. But the most defining moment in his life occurred on September 23, 1908, when Merkle was a nineteen-year-old rookie given a rare start because of an injury to the regular first-baseman, Fred Tenney. Three teams were vying for the pennant and two of them were the New York Giants and the Chicago Cubs. In the bottom of the ninth, the score was tied one to one, with two outs and two Giants on base. Moose McCormick was on third and Merkle was on first. When Al Bridwell hit a single to center field, McCormick crossed the plate for what would have been the winning run, and Giants fans swarmed the field. But something went wrong (and there is considerable debate here). Cubs' manager Frank Chance stormed out of the dugout, screaming for his players to retrieve the ball from center field and tag second base. Chance believed Merkle had gotten lost in the crowd and failed to touch second base. According to the rules, the runner must advance or he could be forced out. When his players finally got the ball to second base, Chance insisted that umpire Hank O'Day call Merkle out, which he promptly did, nullifying the winning run. Since the score was still tied and the fans were still on the field, O'Day declared the game a draw and ordered the teams to replay it at the end of the season. So on October 8, the Giants replayed the Cubs in a game the Giants had earlier won. This time, the Cubs prevailed four to two, and the Giants' season was over. Even though the Giants went on to lose six more games in between Merkle's alleged mistake and the end of the season, angry fans needed someone to blame, and so they pinned the whole season on Merkle. "Don't forget to touch second base," they said whenever they saw him. One member of the media unfairly labeled Merkle a "bone-head" and it stuck. To this day, you can search the Internet for Fred's name and the label "bonehead" will appear next to it.

Described by his manager as "a shrewd and aggressive player," Merkle finished with a lifetime batting average of almost .300 in the days of the "dead ball" and batted in over seven hundred runs. Five times he appeared in the World Series. But, even though any one of us would have done the same thing, Merkle was never forgiven by many for his alleged tragic mistake. Recently, a postscript to the story appeared in *Sports Illustrated.* Thirty years later, Merkle attended a church in Florida with his daughter Marianne, and the visiting minister introduced himself by saying, "You don't know me, but you know where I'm from! Toledo, Ohio! The hometown of Bonehead Fred Merkle." Disappointed by the minister's calloused ignorance, Merkle allegedly whispered to his daughter, "C'mon, let's go," and they slipped out, unnoticed.[1]

I have more than sympathy for Fred Merkle because I have played sports long enough to have made mistakes worse than the one he allegedly made. Many times, on and off the field, I have done something stupid while doing something I was supposed to be good at. Have you?

Why Do Good People Do Bad Things?

Why do people who believe in God, temporarily act as though they do not? As we have seen, the problem is complex because these people really are good, and yet they do not seem to have made an error in judgment so much as revealed a flaw in their character, and you wonder how long that has been there. If they're so good, then why do they do things bad people do? Even if these are mistakes, they must have come from somewhere, so if that's what's coming up in the bucket, you wonder what is down in the well.

Typically, there is a pattern whenever someone blows it. Whenever they are discovered in their sin, there is the initial defense. They deny or rationalize it. But almost invariably, more information is forthcoming. There is a steady flow of juicy details we hadn't heard before, and when they pile up so high, the guilty can no longer deny them. There is the *mea culpa*—the "my fault" or the "Yes, I did it" confession, where they admit they were wrong. When the person is famous, there is usually a press conference and a prepared statement. The confessor is coached, the lines rehearsed, the environment controlled, and there are several questions the guilty cannot answer, because their attorneys will not allow it. You've seen it. The most peculiar component here is the way the confessor distances him- or herself from the sin or separates from the act. It is as though he or she is two different people—the naughty one who committed the act and the virtuous one now confessing it. When the radio host, Don Imus, was confronted for his racial epithets, he deflected the blame by saying, "I did a bad thing but I'm a good person."[2]

After this, the confessors retreat. They drop off the radar. They change jobs or they change churches. They assume a lower profile. The air is too thick with criticism, the scrutiny is too intense, the skepticism too foreboding. They need space. This is not a bad decision, but it is a pivotal one. It is usually in this period, and not in their mea culpa, where it is decided how they will land when it has all blown over. These are crucial hours.

Finally, there is the period of their reemergence. They come out of hiding and join the public again. They are more cautious and contrite, but they are back. The shame has blown over. They guilty are said to have paid their debt to society. Now they can move on.

In every instance, it seems we see a similar process: The person is caught, then defends, then confesses, then retreats, and finally reemerges to start over. The point is, while we have grown cynical about those who once let us down, we still believe in second chances. We even create systems of reentry because we want to know there will be another chance for us if we blow it.

Can the Sick among Us Still Be Holy?

Pretend you are Peter and, like Fred Merkle, you have just come off the worst day of your life. You have a good heart, but sometimes your impulses get you into trouble. You are at the front end of everything. You are the one to walk on water, to pull your taxes out of a fish's mouth, and to cut the soldier with a sword when he comes to take Jesus away. You are the first to speak your mind, to say what others are only thinking: "Lord, explain the parable; it doesn't make sense" or "How many times must we forgive our brother?" When Jesus brings up dying on a cross, only you have the nerve to confront him. Like Merkle, your lifetime batting average is pretty good. But your legacy is marked forever by that one day when you failed to stand up. You let him down. You did something completely opposite your heart's desire. You got blindsided, and overwhelmed and you want, more than anything, not to be remembered for this, but it haunts you after all these years. It's like someone shouting, "Don't forget to touch second base." Your mind replays your greatest hits: "You are the Christ; the Son of the living God" (Matt. 16:16); "Lord . . . tell me to come to you on the water" (14:28); "We have left everything to follow you" (19:27); "Even if all fall away . . . I never will" (26:33). But there is always one more: "I don't know this man you're talking about!" (see 26:69–75).

What a way to go out! We can distance ourselves from Judas because we are not filled with the devil as he was. But we cannot distance ourselves from Peter. We, too, make rash promises one moment and then break them in the next. Out of one heart comes worship and lust. Out of one mouth comes praise and slander. The mind that grasps lofty ideas is sometimes bent on revenge. It turns out Judas and Peter are not that far apart. One betrayed; the other denied. One turned Jesus in for money; the other walked away for fear. One got Jesus arrested; the other would not defend him. Perhaps it is why both men are mentioned in the same chapter in all four gospels, why both received their ominous predictions at the same Last Supper, and why both are victims of Satan. The devil enters one and sifts the other. The wonder is not that Judas hanged himself but that Peter did not.

Matthew is so depressed by Peter's grim failure, he reports it and then never speaks of Peter again. Mark and Luke feel differently. They each stop abruptly in their stories to report that Peter was singled out by Jesus after the resurrection (see Mark 16:7; Luke 24:34). But it is up to John to give us the full account, and he does so in two very moving scenes that are laced with flashbacks—something that allows Peter to look back at his infamous night, to reflect on it and to see it overturned in the present day (see John 21:1–22).

Lord of the Second Chance

So let's say you're a fisherman and you decide to go fishing. Your way of coping with Jesus' death is to try and return to your normal life. Even if Jesus is alive, you're not sure you want to see him anyway, since the last time you saw him, he was staring you in the face after your third denial (see Luke 22:60–62). You and your friends take the boat out and spend the whole evening catching nothing. Early the next morning, you're getting ready to pack it in when you see the figure of someone standing on the shoreline about a hundred yards away.

"You haven't caught any fish, have you?" says the stranger, even though he is too far away to tell. "Throw your net on the right side, and you'll catch something for sure." How it is that this man, standing a football field away, can see the fish on the right side of your boat is beyond you. But so you can say you tried everything, you go ahead and do it. Suddenly, you feel the familiar drag on the nets, and before you know it, you're hauling fish in (see John 21:1–14).

Your mind flashes back three years, to a day when Jesus put himself into your boat and told you to put out into the deep. You complained then, too, that you had fished all night and caught nothing (see Luke 5:4–6). But when you did what he said, you hauled in so many fish that your boat nearly sank.

"Go away from me," you told him, "I am a sinful man" (Luke 5:8). This is how you feel today. Same boat. Same sea. Same story. Nothing has changed. You are just as intense as you've always been, but you don't seem cut out for this. You don't fit the mold.

Now, after your worst day, Jesus is back and he has not given up on you. As you haul in the fish, you know what this means. You are still a fisher of men after all. This is a second chance. The stranger's image is clearer now and John is the first to call it. "It is the Lord!" he screams (John 21:7). As soon as you hear it, you're over the edge of the boat and headed for shore. By the time you get there, Jesus has already started breakfast. He has fish and bread stretched out over a fire.

Your mind flashes back again. It was around a fire, very much like this one, where you gave up on this man (see John 18:18). Now, around the fire, you will get another chance. He is inviting you to eat, and this is no small matter. An invitation to eat is an expression of fellowship and trust. People in our world today miss this, because we frequently eat in restaurants or in our cars and think nothing of the company around us. But on this day, food is scarce. You don't waste it on acquaintances, and you don't eat it alone. It is a way to say the two of you are friends. That is why Jesus is accused of "eat[ing] with tax collectors and 'sinners'" (Matt. 9:11); why he spends his last evening with the disciples by hosting a meal (Mark 14:12–16); and why the insult of Judas' betrayal is ironic. "One of you will betray me," said Jesus at the Last Supper, "one who is eating with me" (Mark 14:18). Eating together is a sign of trust, loyalty, and fellowship. It was at a meal where Jesus predicted you would deny him. Now, at a meal, he will invite you to return. Those who wonder if the sick among us can still be holy need to look intently into this simple act. It is hard to miss what Jesus is saying: "Come, eat with me!"

So as you pull yourself out of the water, Jesus hollers to your friends in the boat, "Bring some of the fish you have just caught" (John 21:10; or some of the fish he just caught). You are beginning to think this moment has been choreographed. Jesus is up to something. To catch what is happening, think of a church potluck. Bob Benson has told how, when he was a college student, he would attend a small church and, from time to time, join them in their potlucks. It was the only way for a college student to get some home cooking. Benson says he had nothing but a bologna sandwich to bring. The good people of that small church surrounded Bob's pathetic looking sandwich with their over-sized menus of fried chicken, baked beans, potato salad, and homemade rolls. "Why don't we just put it all together?" they said. "There's plenty of chicken and plenty of pie and plenty of everything, and we just love baloney sandwiches. Let's put it all together."[3] This is what Jesus is doing. He is putting it all together—yours and his—even though he has plenty of everything. He allows you to participate in something he is already doing. It is as if he is saying, "Yes, you have blown it, but you still have something to add; you have something we can use, something we can share; so bring it with you when you come back."

The Most Important Question

So you stand there for over an hour, eating with the friend you abandoned only a few weeks ago. You talk about fishing, politics, and your family. He asks how your mother-in-law is doing, and you joke about walking on water. But you can tell from the look in his eye there is another conversation he's been waiting to have. There is an elephant in the room and neither you nor he has mentioned it. He is biding time and being polite, but there is unfinished business. In fact, it turns out all of this—the miraculous catch; the fire; the meal; the conversation about news, weather, and sports—is only a prop for the question he will ask you next.

Do you love me?

Three times he asks it. Not one right after the other. There's a lot of chatter in between. But by the end of the morning, he has asked it three times. Perhaps he is giving you three mulligans, one for each time you denied him.[4] Or maybe he just wants to know. Think of it—up to now, no disciple has ever told Jesus he loved him. Isn't that odd? You have walked with him for three years, and it has just now occurred to you that you have never told him this. In fact, the conversations of all the disciples up to now are strangely devoid of this word. People have followed Jesus because they were impressed with his intuitive powers (Nathanael in John 1:50), or because they were directly confronted by Christ (Levi in Mark 2:14), or because they believed in his cause or his mission (James and John in Mark 1:19–20). Some were just caught up in the enthusiasm of Jesus' new movement (the large crowds in Matt. 4:25). But when did these people who came to Christ for other reasons ever decide to love him? Do they love him yet? The synoptic gospels have no one even using the term except for God the Father, Jesus, and a scribe, who is "not far from the kingdom of God."[5] Up to now, the disciples have feared, obeyed, trusted, followed, worshiped, served, and admired him, but they have never said they loved him. Yet, to love the Lord your God with all your heart, soul, mind, and strength is the soul of Christianity (see Mark 12:30).

Do you love me?

It is the most important question. He is not asking you why you did it or whether he can trust you, or how you know it won't happen again. No, these are all questions you would ask if someone was unfaithful to you. But remarkably, these are not the things Jesus wants to know. He does not tell you to repent (even though that is included). He just wants to know:

Do you love me?

And he asks you in the worst possible moment. It is not while you are worshiping, or being baptized, or while you are taking the Eucharist. It is not a question for your Bible study. He is asking you on the heels of a tryst; when your friendship is most strained; when you are least confident. He was right about you. You're not the person you thought you were. You've spent the last two weeks replaying the videos and, just as you start your cyclone down into self-loathing pity, he breaks in to your little world with the question:

Do you love me?

How can you love him when you hate yourself? But he will not take the question away. Do you know why? It is the best form of repentance. You can be sorry without actually loving the person you have hurt. But you will never love without being sorry. It starts with love. When you blow it, it is not sorrow or penance or excuses Jesus wants to draw out of you. It is love. He wants to know when you are most suspicious of your faithfulness if you love him. Do you? There is no question more fundamental than this. Until it is answered, you can go no further. Love, not penance, is the heart and hard work of reconciliation. Love is the motive for all your confessions because love is the standard that calls out the things you confess. Love is the platform for the friendship you will have again once the sin has been absolved.

Do you love me?

The Long Road Home

Each time your response is swift and uncalculated: "Lord, you know I love you." But each time he asks again. If he knows you love him, why does he keep asking? Doesn't he believe you? You start to wonder if you are more convinced than he is, though he is the one who knows all things. Now you're getting nervous. Maybe you have over-estimated yourself again. Maybe you have confused your worship and your God-talk with genuine love. But each time you say it, he has the same response.

"Feed my sheep" (see John 21:17).

What an odd thing to say. Like the question, it is not what you expect. He doesn't say, "Thank you" or "I thought so" or "I love you, too" or make any reference to your answer at all. Instead, he moves right past your confession and says, in effect, "If you love me, feed them." That's when it occurs to you that even though you've done some shameful things—even though you feel disqualified from ever doing something great again—Jesus is not trying to merely reconcile with you. He is not just giving you three do-overs to compensate for your three denials. He is commissioning you. You are standing by the fire where you nearly threw it all away, feeling dirty, and he is saying, "Don't call anything unclean that I have called clean." Now you must rise and go, not in your own power but in his. As he put it so beautifully to the sinful woman you once despised, "Your faith has saved you; go into peace" (Luke 7:50).[6]

Can the sick among us still be holy? It's an important question at the end of a book like this, because peering into the evil that lies buried in us can often leave us feeling dirty. It can overwhelm us and make us want to quit. We keep digging to find the sin behind the sin and sometimes it feels like we will never hit bottom. When will we know all sin is gone? When will we finally get over sin's venom?

How will we know we are not just deceiving ourselves even then? These are all good questions, but they are not the most important. The most important is this:

Do you love Jesus?

If you do, then everything else will come later and in direct proportion to your capacity to love him. If you do, he is inviting you to move from your self-absorption into a larger world of service to others. He is asking you to get involved in what he is doing, to get active in the spiritual lives of others, to care for and nurture someone other than yourself. Sadly, many who are still sick try to assume a new position or return to their old one as though nothing has happened. They want to bring closure to the past by reemerging into positions of chief shepherds before they have learned to feed lambs in small places. They believe once they have found a new place, once other people have accepted them again, their past is over and their restoration is complete. But they fail to realize that love, and not position, is the basis for serving. You do not need a position to serve. Leave that up to the church, and each church will decide the matter differently. You need only a few. You need someone to worry about, to think about, and to pray for besides yourself. You need to be less absorbed in your failure and more absorbed in other people's lives.

I once counseled a woman at the altar who came to confess what she called "a horrible sin."

"What is it?" I asked, but inside I cringed. It had already been a long morning and, by the sound of it, it was about to get even longer.

"I do not love God enough," she said, "and I do not love him aright." At first I breathed a sigh of relief. I was afraid she was going to confess the sin of adultery, or bitterness, or a proud and critical spirit. I was ready for any one of the seven deadly sins. But I was not ready for this. At first, her problem seemed simpler than anything else she could have confessed. Yet, it is the hardest problem to solve. To love God enough and to love him aright is the center of our religion. For want of it, we are vulnerable to every other sin. We may promise, in a moment, to love him, yet it will take us a lifetime to pull it off. But is there anything else? With love, we cover a multitude of sins.

Do you love me?

The question still hangs in the air, two thousand years after Jesus asked it. Only the characters have changed. Like Peter, we gather in circles around the fire every Sunday to eat a meal that Jesus has prepared. He invites us to add what little we have to his abundant supply. He wants us to enjoy him, to say that we love him, and then to move out beyond the fire to those places where he is active in the world. If the sick among us can still be holy, then surely this is the only way. Who would have thought a man once predestined to be the rock of the church would commit a sin as unthinkable as Peter's. Yet who would have thought a man once destined to commit a sin as unthinkable as Peter's would ever become the rock of the church. In fact, both of these moments—Peter's grand confession and stark denial—are wrapped inside the mystery of the church. In it are thousands who are just like Peter, whose fate will not turn on either their grand confession or their unthinkable sin, but on the question put to every disciple at every turn in their lives.

"Do you love me?"

On that question rests our hope.

Study Questions

These study questions are provided to help you review, discuss, and apply the material in each chapter. The questions are designed to be used for personal study first, and then as a guide for small group discussions between four and twelve members.

Prior to group meetings, members should read the chapter to be discussed and wrestle with the study questions on their own, perhaps writing the answers in a personal journal. Then the group can meet to review the material in the chapter and to work through the study questions as a group.

The larger the group, the more difficult it will be to work through all of the questions, so you may decide it's best to break the group down into clusters of two or three to allow you to move through the material more quickly. But remember, the best answers usually come in the last third of any discussion. The first answers are the easiest, and they are usually the least profound. So be sure to allow plenty of time for discussion.

May God truly bless your time together as you admonish, encourage, and pray for one another.

In Pursuit of the Dream
A Passion for Wellness

1. What are your expectations for this book? Why did you decide to read it? What do you hope to get out of it? How will you know, in the end, if it was worth your time and investment?

2. Describe what you think when you hear the word *well*. Give three adjectives to describe a person you would consider well. What, specifically, did you mean by each of those words?

3. A distinction was made between getting better and being well. It is suggested most people want to be well but settle for getting better: "Most people really want to change. They want to be different; they just don't know where to begin. Most people are not rebellious so much as they are stuck" (page 14). Do you agree with this assessment? Why or why not? Do you know anyone who has settled for getting better? How can you tell? What are the symptoms?

4. This book has four underlying assumptions: (1) By God's grace we can develop our virtue even though we are better at vice; (2) Our trouble with sin is not only what it does to our chances of heaven, but what it does to our potential on earth; (3) sin is a very old and clever adversary, and it pursues sinner and saint alike; and (4) sin can be mastered in all of its forms; it can be gotten over and cured in this life. How many of these premises do you agree with? Do you believe it is possible to live without sinning? Why do you think so many people doubt it?

5. How would you define *spiritual transformation*? What does it mean to be transformed? How does it happen? Who are the players? What is the goal? Use as many Scripture references as you can remember or find. Then compare your answers and maybe even modify them as you hear from others in your group.

6. Close by praying, opening yourself to the voice of God's Spirit and asking God to make you well.

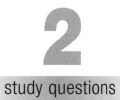

End of Innocence
The Persistence of Vice

1. Which of the seven deadly sins do you think are most tolerated in our culture today? Rank them from one (most tolerated) to seven (least tolerated). Which are most and least tolerated in the church? Give reasons or examples to support your answers. Compare your answers with others in your group.

2. Study again the lists of the deadly sins (or impure thoughts or principle faults) and make as many observations as you can about them. Do you think there is any significance to their order? Do you notice any missing? If you were to modify the list for today, how would you do it?

3. In chapter 2, we learned of a possible third kind of sin called residual sin. In a couple of sentences, summarize what the chapter teaches about residual sin. Write a one-sentence definition you can remember for future reference. Give an example of a residual sin in someone's life.

4. It is suggested that even holy people may sin unknowingly, and that, even though these acts are unintentional, they can still cause problems in our spiritual life. Earlier generations called these weaknesses or infirmities, but here they are called residual sins. What do you like or not like about the term *residual sin*? What do you like or not like about the terms weakness and infirmity? Why do you prefer the one you do? If the discussion in your group gets intense, don't argue. Simply agree to disagree, and move on.

5. In your journal, or with your group, ask God to search your heart for anything that is unbecoming of Christ. Write or pray a prayer of confession, asking God to free you from it.

Flipping the Moon
The Power of Virtue

1. What do you think are some of the most popular, or "pop virtues" in our culture? Don't confine your answers to the seven saving graces but include others. Why are these other virtues so popular? Who decides this for the culture? Where do you see these pop virtues modeled?

2. What virtue do you think God has been trying most to implement in your life over the last few months? How do you know? What or who is he using to do it? What are you doing to cooperate?

3. Chapter 3 compares the sin in our lives to rust on an old classic car and says, "Perhaps God posts a picture on his fridge of what you will look like once he has finished restoring you. For this reason, he paid more to get you than you were worth" (page 44). What does this metaphor do for you? How does it affect your understanding of sin? Of holiness? How could this affect the way you relate to God?

4. Take a few moments to think about the kind of life God may imagine for you. What kind of person do you think he wants you to be? Journal your thoughts or share them with your group. What is keeping you from it? Who do you need to help you with your progress? What part do you want them to play? Write two things you want them to do for you.

5. To "flip the moon," we find the Christian virtue that is most contrary to the sin that entangles us and develop that virtue until our vice has been "flipped" into a virtue. Do you agree with this idea? Have you ever done it? If so, when and how?

First Class Way of Life
Wisdom in Place of *Pride*

1. Some people think you can't be humble and say so. Do you agree? Compare that with Jesus' statement in Matthew 11:29. Can you reconcile Jesus' words with his humility?

2. When did you first notice you were too proud? Can you remember the incident? What did you try to do about it? How effective was your attempt to stifle your pride?

3. Take turns in your group talking about each of the following: (1) a time when you really blew it; (2) something you're not very good at and for which you need the help of others; and (3) a virtue you want in your life but do not have yet, and why.

4. Read over the symptoms of pride again (pages 50–55). Since pride and wisdom are actions as well as attitudes, what is one annoying habit you will try to stop this week (such as, cutting in line, driving aggressively, refusing to admit you're wrong, or talking over the top of others)? Name the annoying habit and tell what you will do to stop it. If you don't know of one, ask the person you live with or someone close to you. They'll name it for sure!

5. What new habit of wisdom will you begin to practice in your daily life? What are some other ways you or your group can think of to practice humility? What will you start doing that leads to humility? Again, if you don't know, ask the members of your group.

Common Cents of Heaven

Hope in Place of *Greed*

1. Who is the most generous person you know? How did he or she become so generous? Was she born that way? Did he learn it over time or did it all come at once? How does she keep generosity in her life? What assumptions do you think he has that most others do not? What sacrifices does he make? What disciplines does he keep? Together with your group, compile a list of attributes generous people share.

2. Chapter 5 says that to Jesus, "money was not a symbol but a lever to get something done. It had no inherent value apart from the opportunities it could create" (page 65). Do you agree with this summary of Jesus' view on possessions? Why or why not? List some of the opportunities you have created for others with your money in the past year or that others have created for you.

3. In chapter 5, we defined greed as (1) "an inordinate desire to possess something" (page 65); (2) "an inordinate love of things or fear of losing them" (page 67); or (3) "our tendency to define our lives and our happiness by our possessions" (page 67). Which of these three expressions of greed resonates most with you? Can you give an example of this expression of greed? What does it look like in someone's life? Share your answers with your group.

4. In a few sentences, explain why hope and not mere generosity is the cure of greed. Write down your brief summary and share it with your group.

5. Imagine someone has given you one hundred fifty thousand dollars with the stipulation that you cannot spend it on yourself. How would you spend it? To whom would you give it? How do you think Jesus would advise you to give it? Pray about your answer. Get advice from others in your group. Then make a list of the people and organizations you would support. Then ask yourself: Are you supporting them now? What would you need to do to align your current support with your proposed one? List one change you can make this week.

What Lies Beneath

Love in Place of *Lust*

1. Of all the deadly sins, lust is often the hardest to confess. Many who struggle with lust have never told anyone about it. Why do you think lust has such a stigma in our culture?

2. Chapter 6 says one cause of our problem with lust is that "our bodies [are] severed from God . . . [and] we leave them behind in our quest to be spiritual" (page 84). As a result, our bodies "grow out of proportion to the rest of our being" (page 85). Do you agree with this assessment? Why or why not? Give examples or evidence to support your answer.

3. Why is love a better cure for lust than self-control or chastity? What examples can you give of someone who does not comprehend true love? What effect do you think this has on his or her struggle with lust? What practical things would you encourage others to do to grow in their capacity to give and to receive true love? Write your answers alone, and then share them with others in your group.

4. Chapter 6 mentions twelve disciplines we may practice to protect ourselves from sin in this area (pages 92–93). How many other practical disciplines can you think of? Interview a few trusted people in your life, asking them the question: "What practical steps do you take to protect yourself from sexual sin?" Make a list of their answers and, together with your own ideas, share this list with your group.

What the Lord Requires

Justice in Place of *Anger*

1. Do you think people are angrier today than past generations? Read
again Peter Wood's description of the "new anger," (pages 96–97).
What examples of "new anger" do you see in our culture?

2. Have you ever thought about what makes you angry? Most people never think about their anger apart from those times when they feel it. So take a few moments to think about the kinds of things that make you angry. Make a list and compare it with others in your group. Notice the similarities and the differences between your list and theirs. What common denominators did you find? What do you think is really behind your anger? What does it teach you about you? If you don't know, ask someone close to you to help. If you dare, share some of your answers with others in your group.

3. Chapter 7 says: "The assumption that life is unfair, that God . . . has picked someone else; that he is no longer punishing evil . . . lies at the bottom of so much of our anger" (page 100). Do you agree? What other things might lie at the bottom of our anger? Look again over your list of things that make you angry. What might you be expecting God to do that he is not doing (such as, making things fairer or stopping people from doing evil things)? Give a specific example of something that has happened in the last week.

4. Look over your list and start thinking about some practical boundaries you can put between you and the situations that make you
   angry. Come up with as many boundaries as you can. Then talk
   with your group through some other possible boundaries you can
   use. Which one of these boundaries will you implement beginning
   this week, and how will you do it? Be specific.

5. Write a prayer confessing your anger to God. Confess your
   weakness and your vulnerability to him, and ask him to protect
   you. In your group, pair up with one other person and pray for
   each other.

Moderation in All Things

Temperance in Place of *Gluttony*

1. Do you think people today have an "obsession with outward beauty and [a] convoluted idea about what beauty is" (page 113)? What is our modern definition of *beautiful*, and where do you think we got it? Do you think our culture is biased for or against overweight people? Support your answer.

2. When it comes to overeating, most of us tend to get in trouble with at least one of the five symptoms (see pages 114–116). Which one of these gives you the hardest time? Rank them according to how often you struggle with them (one, most often; five, least often). Can you give an example from the last couple of weeks in your life? Share these with your group.

3. Chapter 8 says the most insidious form of gluttony is "to crave more from something than it was designed to give" (page 117). What something do you think gluttons crave from their food that their food was not designed to give? Use three different words to answer (such as, security, belonging, peace, or pleasure). Why did you choose those words? Compare your answers to others in your group and make a collective list.

4. Write a one-sentence definition of *temperance*. How is your definition of temperance different from self-control? How is it an antidote for a lifestyle of excess? Write your answers alone, and then discuss them with your group. You may want to modify some of your answers after discussing them.

5. Using your original or modified definition of *temperance* from the previous question, what are some practical things you can do to learn or practice that grace in your life? For instance, what new restraints will you practice? What new limits will you impose? What new discipline will you begin? Pick one and start it this week. Partner with one other person in your group and pray for each other. Then call or e-mail them in three or four days to ask or report on how well you have each followed through.

More than Enough

Faith in Place of *Envy*

1. Where do you most frequently see envy displayed? Is it at work? In sports? In academia? In politics? Give examples from the last couple of weeks.

2. Read Jesus' parable of the workers in the vineyard (Matt. 20:1–16) and put yourself in it. With what group do you most relate: the six o'clock group, the nine o'clock group, or the five o'clock group? Why do you relate with them?

3. Can you think of a place in your life where you fear someone else has more than you? Or where you fear someone else thinks you have more than them? How do you handle that?

4. Chapter 9 makes the argument that faith, not compassion, is the virtue most contrary to envy. In a few sentences, explain the chapter's reason for this (pages 133–136). Do you agree? Look again at the example you gave of someone envying (see question 1 above). Where do you see a lack of faith in that example? Share your answer with the group and have them help you diagnose the example you gave.

5. Make a short list of the things that others have and you want (such as, a better job, a happier marriage, more recognition, or more success). Under each one of these, compile another list of the things you already have in that area (for example, a steady job with an income). Once you have finished, share your list with one other person from your group. Pray for each other, giving thanks to God for what he has already given you out of his generosity.

A Road Less Taken

Courage in Place of *Sloth*

1. What kind of relationship do you think most people today have with their work? Do you think they work too hard or not hard enough? Do you think they love their jobs or not?

2. Early in chapter 10 was a summary of the evolution of our idea of sloth and how the meaning of this word has changed over the years. Which definition comes closest to what you mean when you think of sloth? Where do you think you learned to define it that way?

3. In chapter 10, we learned sloth has many forms. How does sloth, or the fear of it, show itself in your life? Where do you fight it the most? Share with your group how you are tempted and what you do to resist it.

4. Can you think of one project you have started but never finished? What would it take for you to finish that project now? What would be a good next step toward getting it done? When will you start?

5. One way to cure sloth, we have read, is through the practice of a Sabbath. But how is a Sabbath different from a day off? Review some of the components that were included in a Sabbath (see pages 152–153), and contrast these with a typical day off. How are they different? Do you notice anything about your time away from work? Is it more like a Sabbath or a day off? What could you do to implement one of these four components into your next day off?

Back to Eden
In Which We Fell

1. Chapter 11 outlined the four stages many people go through when they blow it: (1) denial, (2) confession, (3) retreat, and (4) reemergence. Take a moment to think of someone, either in the news or in your own life, who has really blown it. Did that person follow this pattern? Where did he or she spend the most time? In your opinion, should he or she have done anything different while moving through the stages?

2. Have you ever blown it? How did you feel? Give two adjectives to describe your condition at that time. If you can, share those adjectives with your group. Be careful to neither counsel one another nor defend yourself by blaming others for your trouble. Just talk about the incident and how you felt about it.

3. When we blow it, "Do you love me?" is the first question Jesus asks us, but it's seldom the question we ask ourselves. What other questions do we ask ourselves that distract us from the main question? Why are these other questions counterproductive?

4. In your opinion, is it possible to love Jesus when you can't love yourself? Is it possible to be truly forgiven, even by God, when we cannot forgive ourselves? Do you know of anyone who has blown it and cannot love or forgive him- or herself? How can you tell? Take a moment and pray for that person, asking God to give him or her an encounter with Jesus like the one Peter had.

5. When you are ready, write a prayer telling God you love him. Be specific. Tell him why. You may want to make a short list of reasons and incorporate them into your prayer.

Notes

Chapter 1

1. The Greek word, *astheneia* means "a want of strength" or an "inability to produce results." (See W. E. Vine, *Vine's Expository Dictionary of Biblical Words*, eds. Merrill F. Unger and William White [Nashville: Thomas Nelson, 1985], 324.) Darrell Bock says that, when referring to human beings it describes arms and legs as "shrunken, withered or wasted." (See Darrell Bock, *The Bible Knowledge Key Word Study: The Gospels* [Colorado Springs: Cook Communications Ministries, 2002], 291.)

2. Walter Brueggemann, *Reverberations of Faith: A Theological Handbook of Old Testament Themes* (Louisville, Ky.: Westminster John Knox, 2002), 83.)

3. Colin Brown, ed., *The New International Dictionary of New Testament Theology*, vol. 2 (Grand Rapids, Mich.: Zondervan, 1986), 169.

4. Gerhard Kittel and Gerhard Friedrich, *Theological Dictionary of the New Testament*, abridged by Geoffrey Bromiley (Grand Rapids, Mich.: Eerdmans Publishing, 1992), 1202.

5. To get an idea of how these two words, *therapeuo* and *hygien*, play against one another, think of the time Jesus healed the man with a withered hand (Matt. 12:10–14) and notice the Pharisee's question, "Is it lawful to *heal* [*therapeuo*, to make better, to improve, to treat, or to cure the disease] on Sabbath?" Then notice Jesus' response: "Stretch out your arm . . . and it was *completely restored* [*hygien*, "made well"] just as sound as the other" (emphasis added).

6. One such question is what the Bible itself teaches. New Testament scholar, Ken Schenck says, "There is no passage in the Bible that assumes a Christian will inevitably sin intentionally when faced with a clear-cut temptation." Source: Personal e-mail to author: December 8, 2009.

7. See John Wesley's sermon "Catholic spirit," *The Works of John Wesley*, vol. V (Grand Rapids: Zondervan, reprinted), 492–504. Wesley pleads for a spirit of unity within diversity: "Though we cannot think alike, may we not love alike? May we not be of one heart, though we are not of one opinion? (493)." Wesley is not suggesting an indifference to doctrine or a "muddy understanding" or a "jumbling [of] all opinions together." To the contrary, the person with the catholic spirit, whose hand I need and seek, "adheres to that worship of God which he judges most acceptable in his sight and, while he is united by the tenderest and closest of ties to one particular congregation, his heart is enlarged toward all mankind; those he knows and those he does not" (503).

8. Robert Mulholland Jr., *Invitation to a Journey* (Downers Grove, Ill.: InterVarsity Press, 1993), 15.

9. Mark Wheeter, (sermon, Wesleyan Woods District Camp, Vassar, Mich., June 29, 2009).

Chapter 2

1. Arthur Falch, letter to the editor, *Christianity Today*, August 2007, 9.

2. Robert E. Sinkewicz, *Evagrius of Pontus: The Greek Ascetic Corpus* (New York: Oxford University Press, 2003), 73.

3. Historian John McNeill writes, "Their authors were not original thinkers, but thoughtful and discriminating legislators of penance and advisers to those charged with the guidance of souls. By their use of ancient materials they helped to maintain in some vigor, through times of violence and moral disorder, the moral force of historic Christianity." John T. McNeill, *A History of the Cure of Souls* (New York: Harper Torchbooks, reprinted 1965), 115.

4. Williston Walker, *A History of the Christian Church,* 4th ed. (New York: Scribner, 1985), 216.

5. Aquinas' work, of some three thousand articles and six hundred questions, is divided into three categories. The first is "the classic explanation of the system of theology held by the Roman Catholic tradition." The other two categories are more pastoral, dealing with virtue and vice and with the use of seven sacraments as conveyers of God's grace. See Earle E. Cairns, *Christianity Through the Centuries*, rev. ed. (Grand Rapids, Mich.: Zondervan, 1967), 258.

6. Dante's use of the seven deadly sins, following Aquinas' list, is very clear but his attaching enemies to each of the sins is only alleged and has not been proven.

7. St. John of the Cross, *Dark Night of the Soul*, trans. and ed. E. Allison Peers (New York: Image Doubleday, reprinted 1990), 37–60.

8. "The Seven New Deadly Sins," www.time.com/time/specials/packages/article/0,28804,1852747_1854195_1854179,00.html (accessed March 10, 2008).

9. Bob Davis, "Lagging Behind the Wealthy, Many Keep Up By Borrowing," *Wall Street Journal*, May 17, 2005.

10. Kurt Anderson, "That was then . . . and this is now," *Time*, April 6, 2009, 34.

11. Ibid.

12. Ron Luce, *Battle Cry for a Generation* (Colorado Springs: NexGen Cook, 2005), 76.

13. David Von Drehle, "The Agitator," *Time*, September 28, 2009, 36.

14. Gloria DeGaetano, "The Impact of Media Violence on Developing Minds and Hearts," in *Childhood Lost: How American Culture is Failing Our Kids*, ed. Sharna Olfman (Westport, Conn.: Praeger, 2005), 93.

15. David Kinnaman, *unChristian: What a New Generation Really Thinks about Christianity . . . and Why It Matters* (Grand Rapids, Mich.: Baker Books, 2007), 54. Parentheses mine.

16. Ibid.

Chapter 3

1. Josef Pieper, *On Hope*, trans. Mary Frances McCarthy (San Francisco: Ignatius, 1986), 25.

2. See *Merriam-Webster New Book of Word Histories* (Springfield, Mass.: Merriam-Webster, Inc., 1991), 496–497.

3. Adrian Hastings, Alistair Mason, and Hugh Pyper, *The Oxford Companion to Christian Thought* (New York: Oxford University Press, 2000), 742.

4. See "Happiness and the Virtues," trans. J. A. K. Thomson, *Vice and Virtue in Everyday Life*, eds. Christina Sommers and Fred Sommers (Belmont, Calif.: Wadsworth Publishing, 2004), 211.

5. J. Oliver Buswell, Jr., *Basic Christian Doctrine*, ed. Carl F. H. Henry (New York: Holt, Rinehart and Winston, 1962), 104.

6. John Calvin, *Insititutes of the Christian Religion,* trans. Ford L. Battles, ed. John T. McNeill, vol. 20–21, *Library of Christian Classics* (Philadelphia: Westminster Press, 1977), 338; cited by David Smith, *With Willful Intent: A Theology of Sin* (Wheaton, Ill.: Victor Books, 1994), 74. Emphasis mine.

7. John Wesley, *The Works of John Wesley*, vol. VI (Grand Rapids, Mich.: Zondervan, 1958–1959), 272.

8. Ibid., 223.

9. John T. McNeill, *A History of the Cure of Souls* (New York: Harper Torchbooks, reprinted 1965), 104.

Chapter 4

1. Clifton Fadiman, ed., *Little Brown Book of Anecdotes* (Boston: Little, Brown and Company, 1985), 454.

2. Gretchen Craft Rubin, *Forty Ways to Look at Winston Churchill: A Brief Account of a Long Life* (New York: Random House, 2004), 87.

3. Robert E. Sinkewicz, *Evagrius of Pontus: The Greek Ascetic Corpus* (New York: Oxford University Press, 2003), 100.

4. Saint Augustine, *Confessions*, II c.6, n.14. Cited by Thomas Aquinas, *On Evil*, trans. John A. Oesterle and Jean T. Oesterle (South Bend, Ind.: University of Notre Dame Press, 1995), 321.

5. Cited by Stanford Lyman, *The Seven Deadly Sins: Society and Evil*, Revised (Dix Hills: General Hall, 1989), 136.

6. William Law, *A Serious Call to a Devout and Holy Life*, ed. John Meister (Philadelphia: Westminster Press, 1955), 108.

7. Ibid., 109.

8. C. S. Lewis, *Mere Christianity* (New York: MacMillan, 1952), 109.

9. Frances de Sales, *Introduction to the Devout Life*, 2nd ed., revised, trans. John K. Ryan (New York: Harper Torchbooks, reprinted 1966), 111.

10. Note, in the text, the shift in the language from *other* to *self*: "They . . . made *themselves* aprons . . . they heard the voice of the LORD [and] . . . hid *themselves* from the presence of the LORD God amongst the trees of the garden" (Gen. 3:7–8 KJV, emphasis added).

11. Wisdom and Folly are the most dominant metaphors in Proverbs and appear in various forms. Wisdom appears as instruction (i.e.: knowledge, correction, and reproof) or as insight (i.e.: understanding and discernment) or as shrewdness and discretion in our dealings with people or things. Folly appears as "the fool" or "the simple" or "the scoffer." See Derek Kidner, *Proverbs* (Tyndale Old Testament Commentary Series) (Downer Grove, Ill.: InterVarsity Press, 1964), 36–42.

12. Steve May, *The Story File* (Peabody, Mass.: Hendrickson, 2000), 246.

13. G. R. Evans, *Bernard of Clairvaux: Selected Works* (Classics of Western Spirituality) (New York: Paulist Press, 1987), 103.

14. Henry Sloan Coffin, *Communion Through Preaching* (New York: Charles Scribner's Sons Ltd., 1952), 16–17, quoted in Ravi Zacharias, *Recapture the Wonder: Experiencing God's Amazing Promise of Childlike Joy* (Nashville: Thomas Nelson, 2003), 16.

15. Evans, *Bernard of Clairvaux*, 100.

Chapter 5

1. E. Randall Floyd, *The Good, The Bad, and the Mad: Some Weird People in American History* (New York: Fall River Press, 2005), 70–74.

2. Howard L. Dayton, Jr., *Your Money Counts* (Longwood, Fla.: Crown Financial Ministries, 1996), 8.

3. Brian S. Rosner, *Greed as Idolatry: The Origin and Meaning of a Pauline Metaphor* (Grand Rapids, Mich.: Eerdmans Publishing, 2007), 123.

4. Thomas Aquinas, *On Evil*, trans. John A. Oesterle and Jean T. Oesterle (South Bend, Ind.: University of Notre Dame Press, 1995), 395.

5. Rosner, *Greed as Idolatry*, 121.

6. Aquinas says an inordinate desire is that in which one desires more than what is sufficient. See Aquinas, *On Evil*, 391.

7. This is an old problem for the elderly. As far back as the Desert Fathers (fourth and fifth centuries), Evagrius warned that greed "suggests to the mind a lengthy old age [with] an inability to perform manual labors [and] famines that are sure to come; sickness that will visit us . . . [and] the great shame that comes from accepting the necessities of life from others." See http://www.ldysinger.com/Evagrius/00_Introd/00a_start.htm.

8. Stanford M. Lyman, *The Seven Deadly Sins: Society and Evil*, rev. ed. (Lanham, Md.: Rowman & Littlefield Publishers, 1989), 235.

9. Tim Kasser, *The High Price of Materialism* (Cambridge, Mass.: MIT Press, 2002), 73.

10. Ibid., 16–17.

11. Donald Gowan, ed. *The Westminster Theological Wordbook of the Bible*, (Louisville, Ky.: Westminster John Knox Press, 2003), 208.

12. Ibid., 211.

13. William T. Cavanaugh, *Being Consumed: Economics and Christian Desire* (Grand Rapids, Mich.: Eerdmans Publishing, 2008), 48.

14. Niall Ferguson, *The Ascent of Money: A Financial History of the World* (New York: Penguin Press, 2008), 27.

15. Ibid., 30.

16. Ibid., 11.

17. Randy Alcorn, *The Treasure Principle: Unlocking the Secret of Joyful Giving* (Sisters, Ore.: Multnomah Books, 2001), 73.

18. This statement has been attributed to the late Father Jean Danielou. Brennan Manning, *The Importance of Being Foolish: How to Think Like Jesus* (San Francisco: HarperOne, 2005), 13.

19. My father has provided me with a helpful list of almost eighty verses on money in the book of Proverbs. For those who chase money, see Proverbs 11:4; 23:4; 28:20, 22. For those who share possessions, see Proverbs 11:25; 19:17; 22:9; 28:27.

20. Malcolm Muggeridge, *Something Beautiful for God, Mother Teresa of Calcutta* (New York: Harper & Row, 1971), 32.

Chapter 6

1. Lust, or *luxuria* as it was called by the early church, means an overpowering, inordinate desire for something—whether power, fame, prosperity, success—but as these are often included in other deadly sins, the term *lust* has been historically applied to sexual desire. That is the meaning in this chapter as well.

2. An online survey asked, "Of the seven deadly sins [which] one is your biggest failing?" Lust was cited by 31 percent of the respondents. The others sins were as follows: anger (20 percent), pride (18 percent), sloth (13 percent), gluttony (8 percent), greed (5 percent), and envy (5 percent). Figures were updated October 25, 2009. See http://whitestonejournal.com/index.php/seven-deadly-sins.

3. Ann Oldenburg, "Study says there is more sex on TV," *USA Today*, November 9, 2005, cited in "Leading Sexual Indicators," *Leadership Journal*, Winter 2006, 35.

4. C. S. Lewis, *Mere Christianity* (New York: MacMillian Co., 1960), 89.

5. Rutgers University, www.rutgers.edu/Publications/SourcesThings4teens.htm, cited in "Leading Sexual Indicators," *Leadership Journal*, Winter 2006, 35.

6. Diane Levin, *Childhood Lost: How American Culture is Failing Our Kids* (Santa Barbara, Calif.: Praeger, 2005), 138, 146.

7. "237 Reasons to Have Sex," cited in *Leadership Journal*, Winter 2008, 60.

8. John W. Kennedy, "Help for the Sexually Desperate," *Christianity Today*, March 2008, 30.

9. Ibid., 32.

10. Philip Yancey, *Rumors of Another World: What on Earth Are We Missing?* (Grand Rapids, Mich.: Zondervan, 2003), 79.

11. The survey that produced this alarming statistic included all couples, married or unmarried. See Frank Luntz, *What Americans Really Want . . . Really: The Truth about our Hopes, Dreams and Fears* (New York: Hyperion, 2009), 43.

12. W. E. Vine, *Vine's Expository Dictionary of Biblical Words*, eds. Merrill F. Unger and William White (Nashville: Thomas Nelson, 1985), 353.

13. Lynne Luciano, *Looking Good: Male Body Image in Modern America* (New York: Hill & Wang, 2001), 3–4.
14. Ann Woods, "The New Rules of Sex," *Marie Claire*, February 2007, 75.
15. Thomas Merton, *No Man Is an Island* (New York: Harvest HBJ, 1983), 3–4.

Chapter 7

1. From the journal of Walter Trumbull, a member of the Washburn Expedition of 1870. See: http://www.yellowstone-online.com/history/trumbull/ trumbull13.html (accessed December 4, 2009).
2. "Geyser-eruptions, types of geysers, numbers and distribution, misnamed geysers, geysers on Triton," http://www.encyclopedia.stateuniversity.com/ pages/8672/geyser.html (accessed June 18, 2009).
3. Recently a Harvard study on IED revealed that 7.3 percent of Americans have experienced some form of IED in the past year, a figure that was much higher than researchers imagined. While the definition is not precise, and allows for milder forms of anger, most researchers agree that today, anger is more pronounced and widespread. See http://www.thehindu.com/ 2006/06/09/ stories/2006060905481100.htm (accessed December 4, 2009).
4. Peter Wood, *A Bee in the Mouth: Anger in America Now* (New York: Encounter Books, 2007), 23.
5. Ibid., 24–25.
6. Robert E. Sinkewicz, *Evagrius of Pontus: The Greek Ascetic Corpus* (New York: Oxford University Press, 2003), 80.
7. Thomas Aquinas, *On Evil*, trans. John A. Oesterle and Jean T. Oesterle (South Bend, Ind.: University of Notre Dame Press, 1995), 372.
8. St. John of the Cross, *Dark Night of the Soul*, trans. and ed. E. Allison Peers (New York: Image Doubleday, reprinted 1990), 53.
9. This phrase is taken from John Steinbeck's novel *East of Eden*, and cited by Walt Bruegemann, *Genesis: Interpretation: A Bible Commentary for Teaching and Preaching* (Atlanta: John Knox, 1982), 55.
10. Robert Shemin, *How Come That Idiot's Rich and I'm Not?* (New York: Three Rivers Press, 2009).
11. John Ortberg, "The Sin-Tamer," *Leadership Journal*, Spring 2009, 34.
12. Gerard Reed, *C. S. Lewis Explores Vice and Virtue* (Kansas City, Mo.: Beacon Hill Press, 2001), 45.

Chapter 8

1. International Federation of Competitive Eating, http://www.ifoce.com/ eaters.php?action=detail&sn=22.
2. Ibid.
3. Victorino Matus, "The Sin We Stomach Best," http://www.beliefnet.com/ News/2002/03/The-Sin-We-Stomach-Best.aspx (accessed December 16, 2009).
4. "Glutton," in *Chambers Dictionary of Etymology*, ed. Robert K. Barnhard (New York: Chambers-Harrop, reprinted 2004), 438.
5. Stanford M. Lyman, *The Seven Deadly Sins: Society and Evil*, rev. ed. (Lanham, Md.: Rowman & Littlefield Publishers, 1989), 222.
6. "Canonical Definitions," www.evagrius.net/readarticle.php?article_id=2.

7. Peter Kreeft, *Back to Virtue: Traditional Moral Wisdom for Modern Moral Confusion* (San Francisco: Ignatius Press, 1992), 177.

8. Ibid., 66.

9. Augustine, *Confessions* X, cited by Thomas Aquinas, *On Evil*, trans. John A. Oesterle and Jean T. Oesterle (South Bend, Ind.: University of Notre Dame Press, 1995), 415.

10. Gregory, *Moralia,* XXX, cited by Aquinas, *On Evil*, 419.

11. Timothy Lamer, "Branding Children," *World*, August 18, 2007, 51.

12. Cited by Aquinas, *On Evil*, 419.

13. Ibid.

14. Cited by Gerard Reed, *C. S. Lewis Explores Vice and Virtue* (Kansas City, Mo.: Beacon Hill Press, 2001), 68.

15. Ibid.

16. Ken Bazyn, *The Seven Perennial Sins and Their Offspring* (New York: Continuum, 2004), 144.

17. C. S. Lewis, *The Lion, the Witch and the Wardrobe* (Chronicles of Narnia) (New York: HarperCollins, 2005), 34–35.

18. Written by my son, Nicholas DeNeff, in an unpublished manuscript on the Seven Deadly Sins (2007).

19. For on interesting study of this written in the language of those who, like me, are unfamiliar with the science, see Jonah Lehrer, *How We Decide* (New York: Houghton Mifflin, 2009).

20. Karl Barth, *The Humanity of God* (Richmond, Va.: John Knox, 1960), 46.

21. Ibid., 50.

22. Lori Oliwenstein, "Weighty Issues," *Time*, June 23, 2008, 101.

23. Lyman, *The Seven Deadly Sins*, 225–230.

24. Cited by Bazyn, *Seven Perennial Sins*, 150.

25. H. E. Jacobs, "Temperance," *International Standard Biblical Encyclopedia*, ed. James Orr (Chicago: Howard-Severance Co., 1915), 2929. Emphasis added.

Chapter 9

1. Thomas Aquinas, *On Evil*, trans. John A. Oesterle and Jean T. Oesterle (South Bend, Ind.: University of Notre Dame Press, 1995), 356.

2. Peter Kreeft, *Back to Virtue: Traditional Moral Wisdom for Modern Moral Confusion* (San Francisco: Ignatius Press, 1992), 122.

3. See Jean Delumeau, *Sin and Fear: The Emergence of a Western Guilt Culture, 13–18th Centuries*, trans. Eric Nicholson (New York: St. Martin's Press, 1990), 428.

4. Cornelius Plantinga, *Not the Way It's Supposed to Be: A Breviary of Sin* (Grand Rapids, Mich.: Eerdmans Publishing, 1995), 171.

5. Kreeft says, "We are commanded to 'rejoice with those who rejoice and weep with those who weep' [but] envy is not *with* but *at*. It weeps at those who rejoice and rejoices at those who weep. It refuses the primal fact of the family, the body . . . It enacts the falsehood of alienation instead of the truth of solidarity," *Back to Virtue*, 123–124.

6. Gordon MacDonald, *Restoring Your Spiritual Passion* (Nashville: Thomas Nelson, 1986), 99.

7. Nat Shapiro, *Whatever It Is, I'm Against It* (New York: Simon & Schuster, 1984), 84, cited in James B. Simpson, ed., *Webster's II New Riverside Desk Quotations* (Boston: Houghton-Mifflin, 1992), 200.

8. C. S. Lewis, "Screwtape Proposes a Toast" in *The Screwtape Letters* (New York: MacMillan, reprint 1961), 162.

10. Helmut Schoeck, *Envy: A Theory of Social Behaviour* (Indianapolis, Ind.: Liberty Fund, Inc., 1987).

11. I am indebted to my friend Jeff Fussner for introducing me to Foster's work and for summarizing it so plainly in his doctoral dissertation, from which I have borrowed these concepts.

12. Joseph Telushkin, *Book of Jewish Wisdom: Ethical, Spiritual and Historical Lessons from the Great Works and Thinkers* (New York: William Morrow, 1994), 202.

13. George Foster, "The Anatomy of Evil: A Study in Symbolic Behavior." *Current Anthropology* 13 (1972): 165–200.

14. Cornelius Plantinga, Jr., *Not the Way It's Supposed to Be: A Breviary of Sin* (Grand Rapids, Mich.: Eerdmans Publishing, 1995), 168.

15. H. G. Wells, *Dictionary of Humorous Quotations*, ed. Evan Esar (New York: Bramhall House, 1949), 213.

Chapter 10

1. Charles R. Swindoll, *Living on the Ragged Edge: Coming to Terms with Reality* (Waco, Tex.: Word Books, 1985), 24.

2. Dorothy L. Sayers, *Creed or Chaos?: Why Christians Must Choose Either Dogma or Disaster (Or , Why It Really Does Matter What You Believe)*, (Manchester, N.H.: Sohpia Institute Press, 1999), 110.

3. Robert E. Sinkewicz, *Evagrius of Pontus: The Greek Ascetic Corpus* (New York: Oxford University Press, 2003), 99.

4. Gregory the Great, *Pastoral Rule*, The Nicene and Post-Nicene Fathers, second series, ed. Phillip Schaff and Henry Wace (Grand Rapids, Mich.: Eerdmans Publishing, 1952–1957), 39.

5. Ken Bazyn, *The Seven Perennial Sins and Their Offspring* (New York: Continuum, 2004), 162.

6. Thomas Aquinas, *On Evil*, trans. John A. Oesterle and Jean T. Oesterle (South Bend, Ind.: University of Notre Dame Press, 1995), 361–362.

7. St. John of the Cross, *Dark Night of the Soul*, trans. and ed. E. Allison Peers (New York: Image Doubleday, reprinted 1990), 60.

8. A.W. Tozer, *The Root of the Righteous* (Harrisburg, Pa.: Christian Publications, 1955), 55.

9. Peter Kreeft, *Back to Virtue: Traditional Moral Wisdom for Modern Moral Confusion* (San Francisco: Ignatius Press, 1992), 155–156.

10. Gregory, *Pastoral Rule*, 39.

11. Derek Kidner, *Proverbs* (Tyndale Old Testament Commentaries) (Downers Grove, Ill.: InterVarsity Press, 1964), 42.

12. Sayers, *Creed or Chaos?*, 109.

13. Bazyn, *The Seven Perennial Sins*, 162.

14. Ibid.

15. Sayers, *Creed or Chaos?*, 108.
16. Mary Wilson Little in Evan Esar, *Dictionary of Humorous Quotations* (New York: Bramhall House, 1949), 132.
17. John Wesley, *The Works of John Wesley*, vol. VII (Grand Rapids, Mich.: Zondervan, reprinted), 406.
18. Marva Dawn, *Keeping the Sabbath Wholly: Ceasing, Resting, Embracing , Feasting* (Grand Rapids, Mich.: Eerdmans Publishing, 1989).
19. Brian Tracy, *Eat that Frog! 21 Great Ways to Stop Procrastinating and Get More Done in Less Time* (San Francisco: Berrett-Koehler Publishers, 2002).

Chapter 11

1. Keith Olberman, "The Goof that Changed the Game," *Sports Illustrated*, September 23, 2008.
2. "Transcript: Imus puts remark into context," http://www.msnbc.msn.com/id/18022596/page/2 (accessed August 20, 2009).
3. Bob Benson, *Stories From the Heart*, ed. Alice Gray (Portland, Ore.: Multnomah, 2000), 198.
4. This is perhaps the most common explanation for Jesus repeating the question, and undoubtedly, this is not lost on Peter. But this only explains why Jesus raised the question three times. It does not explain why he raised the question at all and not another. The most common answer is that Jesus and Peter are using different Greek words for "love;" Jesus using the word *agape* ("Do you love me with an unfailing love?") and Peter replying each time with the word *phileo* ("Yes, Lord, we are friends!"). While this theory does point to a distinction between the two Greek words for "love," it "fails to notice John's habit to introduce slight variation in repetitions . . . without appreciable difference of meaning." See Leon Morris, *The Gospel According to John*, rev., *The New International Commentary on the New Testament* (Grand Rapids, Mich.: Eerdmans Publishing, 1995), 769.
5. The scribe who used the term only reiterated what Jesus had said, "You are right . . . To [love the Lord your God] . . . is more important than all the burnt offerings and sacrifices" (Mark 12:32–33), and still for his answer, he is told that he is "not far from the kingdom of God" (Mark 12:34).
6. The Simon in this story is surely a different one than Peter, though Peter likely felt the same as the Pharisee in this story.